Praise for *The Am*

"Mizejewski reads *The Americans* as a domestic melodrama that negotiates the terrain of the real and the 'real.' It is an incisive analysis informed by her immersion in all aspects of '80s history and culture."

—Ina Rae Hark, University of South Carolina

"While *The Americans* has earned its place in television history as a phenomenal spy show, Linda Mizejewski demonstrates, in a series of compelling and lucid arguments, how its originality is indebted to its particular orchestration of elements from domestic family melodrama, including its portrayal of gender, family, children, and the nation. In exploring the intersection of the spy genre and family melodrama, Mizejewski has given us a terrifically insightful and teachable book that helps us to appreciate *The Americans* as one of the most morally complex and challenging of television dramas in recent memory."

—Barbara Klinger, Indiana University

"With her nuanced analysis Mizejewski makes clear just what is so distinctive about *The Americans:* its fusing of espionage and domestic melodrama, its involvement of children in espionage, and most of all its challenging positioning of the series' spectators in morally ambiguous and complex ways. A great book on a provocative and innovative show."

—Diane Waldman, Associate Professor Emerita, University of Denver

"*The Americans* is both gripping and groundbreaking, and there is no scholar more astute and no author more adroit than Linda Mizejewski. Her writing is just as captivating as the show itself. This is no small achievement, particularly because *The Americans* is smart and well written and requires that any scholar bring her 'A game' to its consideration. Fortunately, Mizejewski's work is *always* excellent. Indeed, Linda Mizejewki is one of the finest writers publishing in gender and media analysis today, and it is a true pleasure to spend time with her and her insights in this book."

—Brenda R. Weber, Provost Professor and Jean C. Robinson Scholar at Indiana University

The Americans

TV Milestones

Series Editor

Barry Keith Grant, Brock University

TV Milestones is part of the Contemporary Approaches to Film and Media Series.

A complete listing of the books in this series can be found online at wsupress.wayne.edu.

The Americans

Linda Mizejewski

Wayne State University Press
Detroit

Manufactured in the United States of America.

Library of Congress Control Number: 2021943147

ISBN (paperback): 978-0-8143-4743-0
ISBN (ebook): 978-0-8143-4744-7

Wayne State University Press rests on Waawiyaataanong, also referred to as Detroit, the ancestral and contemporary homeland of the Three Fires Confederacy. These sovereign lands were granted by the Ojibwe, Odawa, Potawatomi, and Wyandot nations, in 1807, through the Treaty of Detroit. Wayne State University Press affirms Indigenous sovereignty and honors all tribes with a connection to Detroit. With our Native neighbors, the press works to advance educational equity and promote a better future for the earth and all people.

Wayne State University Press
Leonard N. Simons Building
4809 Woodward Avenue
Detroit, Michigan 48201-1309

Visit us online at wsupress.wayne.edu

CONTENTS

ACKNOWLEDGMENTS

I owe a great deal of gratitude to my Society of Cinema and Media Studies friends and colleagues whose insights and impassioned conversations guided and inspired this book. Allison McCracken and Joe Wlodarz were brilliant coordinators of our lively *Americans* seminar, which included Laure Astourian, Ina Rae Hark, Lillian Holman, Lisa Jacobson, Barbara Klinger, Thais Miller, Daisy Pignetti, Diane Waldman, and Anna Varadi, most of whom were willing to show up in wigs and other disguises so that we could, paradoxically, "make it real." Brenda Weber joined some of us for a follow-up panel, and later I was fortunate enough to have both Brenda and Allison McCracken as the press reviewers for this manuscript. Their thoughtful and perceptive readings and suggestions very much influenced my revisions and made this a much stronger TV Milestones offering. My thanks also to Judith Mayne, who talked me into doing this book, and to Gillian Silverman and Sarah Hagelin, who shared their own work on *The Americans*. It was a thrill to work with all these scholars who love this series as much I do. Marie Sweetman at Wayne State University Press was with me all the way, making the book possible and a lot of fun. And as always,

George Bauman supported and loved me all through this project. Our time together behind the Iron Curtain is part of our unending bond, and it was especially meaningful to watch and think about this Cold War television series with him. Thanks, babe!

INTRODUCTION

The Cold War and Homemade Brownies

Upstairs, Downstairs

Joe Weisberg, the creator of *The Americans* (FX 2013–18), experienced the Cold War as I did, in 1980s Soviet-bloc Romania, where I was a Fulbright lecturer. My husband and I were the Americans—literally, the only ones—in the small northern city where I was teaching. We were aware that a shadow life of deception, secrecy, and surveillance imbued all our friendships and interactions with the locals, who were required to report all conversations with us to Securitate, the secret police. A Romanian once whispered to us, "You don't know half of what's going on around you, and it's best that you don't." In our apartment, we would often gesture to the wobbly ceiling-light fixture because we'd learned in spy movies that it was where the microphone was likely installed. But it could also have been just a wobbly fixture. It had the same effect either way. Our Romanian friends—the ones preapproved by Securitate—would ring the doorbell and beckon us into the hallway if they had something important to say.

My secret-police file resides in Bucharest with personal details of our nine months there. It was included as material for a 2013 study by a Romanian historian describing how Fulbrighters were unwittingly caught up in the constraints, contrivances, and surveillance practices of everyday life in a totalitarian state (Liviu-Marius 2013).[1] Even given the details in that article, I'll never know how much of what we experienced—the friendships, the confidences, the colleagueship—was real and how much was staged. Also disconcerting was our realization that American operations in the Cold War were just as underhanded. We had laughed at Romanian accusations that some of the Fulbrighters were spies, but we gradually developed suspicions.

I like to imagine that I brushed past Joe Weisberg in Bucharest at one of those "grand restaurant[s] without food" that he describes (Rice 2017), but our connection actually happens in my engagement, as fan and critic, with the television series he developed nearly thirty years later. Weisberg had traveled to Romania in the 1980s after he graduated from Yale, and the authoritarian world he saw inspired him to join the CIA and become an undercover operative. By the time he left the agency in 1993, the Soviet Union had dissolved, and he had become disillusioned about the ethics of American intelligence operations. He also learned how deception can become a way of life. "I lied every day," he reports. "I told 20 lies a day and I got used to it. It was hard for about two weeks. Then it got easy" (Holson 2013).

The surreal nature of deception as a way of life is central to Weisberg's series *The Americans*, cowritten with Joel Fields, which ran six seasons after its debut on FX in 2013. *The Americans* is based on the KGB's "illegals" program of the 1980s, which sent Soviet agents to live in the United States as American citizens and gather intelligence from contacts in their government or industry jobs. The program made headlines in 2010 when the FBI arrested a number of illegals who were still living as suburban American couples in northern Virginia,

1 The file also includes Securitate's response to my own published reflection (Mizejewski 1987) on that experience.

New York, and Boston (see McGreal 2010; Shane and Savage 2010).[2] This astonishing story of Soviet-constructed suburbanites was a perfect match for Weisberg's expertise as a writer and a former operative. He and Fields developed protagonists Philip and Elizabeth Jennings (Matthew Rhys and Keri Russell) who are "Americans" rather than Americans—Russian spies posing as middlebrow travel agents in a suburb of Washington, DC, with their two children.

The Americans transfigured television history with its bold merger of the spy genre and domestic melodrama. Early in the pilot episode, Philip locks a kidnapped victim, a Soviet defector, into the trunk of the family car and then takes a few steps from the attached garage to the kitchen where he helps the kids clean up breakfast and figure out rides to school. The other uncanny space in the house is the basement. In a jarring version of the Masterpiece Theater upstairs-downstairs formula, it's the dark, adjoining space of illicit activity where the Jenningses keep their secret stash of wigs, passports, guns, and spy apparatuses, like recording devices and disappearing ink. So the house itself literalizes the contiguous spaces of family life and espionage, as well as the perils of this intimate arrangement. By the end of the first season, the Jenningses' daughter, Paige (Holly Taylor), starts snooping in the basement, and in later seasons, it's where her mother trains her in self-defense, having recruited her into a new program for second-generation KGB illegals.

As a spy series spun around the axis of marriage and suburban domestic life, *The Americans* explores questions of loyalty, patriotism, deception, and violence through the prisms of family and gender roles. The breathtaking action sequences and suspenseful undercover operations, set to the rhythms of 1980s rock music, provide the spy-genre thrills. But the emotional scenes that bond viewers to the characters

2 For an account of two young men discovering their "American" parents were Russian spies, see Shaun Walker (2016). The most famous of the illegals was Jack Barsky, who appeared on American news shows and wrote a memoir about his experience (2017).

are set in the locations of soap opera—the kitchen, the bedrooms, and the family room where the Jenningses watch a David Copperfield magic special on television. These family scenes resonate with chilling implications. The recruitment of a teenager into the KGB is alarming, but it also stirs up uncomfortable questions about how children are more subtly recruited into their parents' belief systems and into prevalent ideologies. This series matters—in cultural and television history—because of this discomfiting exploration of 1980s suburban life as a microcosm of the moral complexities of Americanism.

Tapping political, cultural, and clandestine histories, *The Americans'* producers painstakingly re-created 1980s American life and espionage techniques. The costume designers combed vintage stores for high-waist trousers and boxy blazers, and the writing staff studied 1980s TV schedules to ensure the accuracy of what could appear on a television set in the background on a given night of the week. Props specialists tracked down antiquated espionage items from a collector who provided a miniature camera actually used by the KGB, and the CIA scrutinized every script for sensitive details that might have repercussions.[3] But the props were often objects charged with other meanings. In the pilot episode, Philip is at a mall coveting cowboy boots in a shoe display and thinking that being an American wouldn't be so bad. When he says so to Elizabeth, she slaps his face for the treachery. But he's already bought the boots. Later in the pilot, the Jenningses argue about how they can raise their children to be socialists in a materialist culture. However, this episode also shows, in flashback, their awe at a motel window air conditioner when they arrive in Virginia from the Soviet Union on a hot summer night. Philip's first impression of the United States, he says, is that it's "brighter" here. Details like this—cowboy boots, a window air conditioner, electrical

3 These details are included in the Slate podcast *The Americans* for season 3, episodes 1 and 2. These podcasts are cited hereafter as podcast, season number, episode number.

wattage—show up throughout *The Americans* as the everyday material that shapes and symbolizes conflicts about identity, loyalty, and citizenship.

These conflicts confront audiences, too, muddying who they should root for in the spy-versus-spy chases—the "real" Americans of the FBI or the faux "Americans" who are the main characters. The pilot begins with a honey-trap sex scene of a dolled-up Elizabeth with a duped Department of Justice official. Elizabeth is so obviously playing dumb and the official is so easily manipulated that it's impossible for viewer sympathy to come down on his side. From the first, we're positioned within the Soviet side of the Cold War. Weisberg says the KGB, reviled in the United States as the epitome of what Ronald Reagan called "an evil empire," was regarded as a prestigious and patriotic organization in the USSR, far removed from the rampant corruption elsewhere in the regime (Rice 2017). In *The Americans*, this prestige is reflected in the richly appointed Rezidentura, the KGB office complex at the Soviet embassy. Its lush woodwork, linen lampshades, and brocade tapestries offer a vivid contrast to the sterile offices of the FBI. The office politics and romances inside the Rezidentura are rendered in the same depth as those of their American counterparts. And we see Soviet failures, like the occupation of Afghanistan, through the perspective of characters we care about. Russian actors play out entire scenes in their native language with English subtitles, amplifying the series' outsider perspective on American culture.

Perhaps most unsettling for viewer expectations are protagonists who are actively trying to take down the United States, which is a stretch even for television's ongoing run of gritty antiheroes. Elizabeth and Philip kill not only their espionage opponents but sometimes innocents and bystanders as well—an old woman who shows up in the wrong place and time, a lab worker whose research on world hunger is disastrously misunderstood. But the Jenningses are also appealing characters whose stories of marriage, partnership, intimacy, and parenthood are the heart of every episode. Critics, reviewers, and the writers themselves often remarked that *The Americans* was as much about marriage as about espionage, with the Cold War serving as a metaphor for marital divides, standoffs, and uneasy détente.[4]

The pilot stunningly enacts this metaphor, halfway through the episode, with a close-up shot of Elizabeth and Philip angrily clutching a large gleaming kitchen knife between them. Elizabeth has impatiently rebuffed Philip's kisses as they stand at the kitchen counter where she's cutting homemade brownies for their new neighbors. When he persists, she whips around with the knife toward his throat, but Philip—equally an expert in martial arts—just as quickly catches her hand. "You're my wife," he hisses. "Is that right?" she retorts. The marital embrace in the kitchen—a cliché of television series about suburban families—becomes a standoff between two highly trained KGB agents, literally at each other's throats. And it allows Elizabeth's question about the nature of marriage to echo through the pilot and through the series, given that the Jenningses' marriage, far from being sanctioned by either church or state, was a KGB arrangement for their assignment in the illegals program.

In turn, the questions about "real" marriage expand throughout *The Americans* to questions about what makes identity, family, citizenship, and home "real." One of Philip's kidnapped victims taunts him in an episode in season 2: "You'll go home to your family. Is 'home' the right word? . . . Your name isn't your name, is it? Is your face your face? Are your children your children?" ("The Deal" 2.5). Both Philip and Elizabeth have multiple names and faces, and their KGB handler tells them at one point that their children are not in fact their own but belong to the state.

---

4 See, for example, the Joel Fields interview in which he says, "In every episode, we asked ourselves, 'What's the marriage story?' It doesn't matter if the spy story is working; we've got to have the marriage story working" (Keller 2016). For examples of commentary on the centrality of the marital conflict in this series from a variety of sources, see Olivia Armstrong (2015), Joshua Rothman (2016), *State Journal Register* (2013), and James Poniewozik (2015).

Philip (Matthew Rhys) and Elizabeth (Keri Russell) grapple with a kitchen knife in a shot that captures the series' merger of domestic melodrama and espionage violence.

Soul searching and melodramatic quandary are not new to the spy genre. From John le Carré's novels to television dramas such as *The Bureau* (Oligarchs/Canal [France] 2015–), *Berlin Station* (Epix 2016–19), and *The Spy* (Netflix 2019), espionage protagonists confront ethical crises within flawed institutions—British Military Intelligence, the CIA, Mossad—that demand compromising behavior. Moral interrogation is intrinsic to melodrama in its broadest meaning as storytelling about the individual caught up in crises of conscience, obligation, class, race, family, or community. In his foundational work on melodrama, Peter Brooks emphasizes that it is a way of "making the world morally legible" (1976, 42). And like most popular narrative formulas, from the Western to the war narrative to the sports drama, the spy genre usually tells its stories by drawing on melodrama's tropes of emotional confrontations, plots driven by crisis and sudden reversals, and extremes of villainy and virtue.

The originality of *The Americans*, though, is that it's grounded more specifically in *domestic* melodrama. Philip's kidnapped victim gets to him because he needles him about home and children. Often dismissed as lesser, "feminine" types of drama—soap opera, the chick flick, the "woman's film"—these stories about family, marriage, and relationships nevertheless often feature men's stories, too, as evident in the popular NBC series *This Is Us* (2016–) that overlapped with the run of *The Americans*. Domestic melodrama is driven by conflicts around gender roles, whether or not men are the focus, so it often highlights the contradictions of patriarchy and heterosexuality, as seen in the Jenningses' mimicry of a traditional family in which Elizabeth's primary roles are supposed to be wife and mother.[5] But the overwhelming appeal to female audiences for melodrama is that it takes women's emotional lives seriously. *The Americans*' pilot episode dramatizes the double binds of female experience when it shifts focus to Elizabeth as a rape survivor. We learn that while she was being trained as a young cadet in Moscow, she was sexually assaulted by her KGB commander, who felt it was a perk of the job. Elizabeth has been silent about this for almost twenty years. As the #MeToo movement has proven, silence is a common response of women doubly victimized by the trauma of the rape and by shame—in this case, further complicated by Elizabeth's anger that the KGB had betrayed her.

Elizabeth's sexual-assault experience is the fulcrum on which the entire pilot episode rests. Soon we learn that the kidnapped defector in their garage is her rapist, whom the Jenningses are ordered to turn over safely to their Soviet colleagues. Once viewers know this, the reason for Elizabeth's coldness toward Philip's physical advances in this episode snaps into place. She's revisiting the trauma and doesn't want to be touched. When she finally discloses the whole story to Philip, he

5 Linda Williams points out the cultural biases about melodrama and makes the case for melodrama as the norm of Hollywood cinema (2001, 16–23). Also see Gledhill (2018), who argues for the wider significance of melodrama as an aesthetic mode that crosses genres and national cultures. Feminist scholars have long been interested in the domestic or family melodrama as a site where women's suffering is privileged (see, for example, Karlyn 1995; Haskell 1999; Levine 2018).

kills the defector with his bare hands, disobeying their KGB orders and scuttling the assignment. It could be argued that Philip's heroics undermine Elizabeth's own revenge story and establish him as her avenger rather than her partner. But Elizabeth doesn't need an avenger; she beats the defector senseless and kicks his head through a wall before Philip delivers the fatal twist. What she needs instead is evidence that Philip's loyalty lies first with her rather than with the KGB. It's the turning point of the episode and of their emotional lives. After their expert disposal of the body near an industrial site outside the city, Elizabeth initiates passionate sex in the front seat of their car, and shortly thereafter, in a tender scene in bed, she finally tells Philip her Russian first name: "My name is—was—Nadezhda." The rape story line of the pilot episode illustrates how *The Americans* maps the female concerns of domestic melodrama onto the plots of KGB espionage.

But the male melodrama in this series is no less compelling.[6] *The Americans* vividly depicts the emotional lives of its male characters, especially of Philip Jennings as he struggles with his conflicts as an agent, husband, father, friend, and lover. Just before he kills the defector in the basement, he attends a patriotic middle-school event with his young son, and the camera closes in on his stricken face as he watches the miniature flags waving around him and realizes his son is, obviously but ironically, an American. For his own part, Philip's attraction to American culture galvanizes his character from the start, signaled by that covetous gaze at the cowboy boots. The more "American" of the Jennings couple, Philip is a figuration of ex-CIA showrunner Weisberg himself, the agent who became cynical about his work and cause.

6 As Tania Modleski (2010) has pointed out, narratives about male suffering have always been privileged as "tragedy" or "drama," whereas stories of female suffering get denigrated as "soaps" or chick flicks. See also Sklar and Modleski (2005). You can see the bias about the term *melodrama* in the way it is excised in discourses about the prestigious male dramas of "quality television"—*The Sopranos* (HBO 1999–2007), *Breaking Bad* (AMC 2008–13), *Mad Men* (AMC 2005–15).

Up against the steadfast KGB loyalty of his wife, Philip's discontent is the fault line of their marriage.

The fully drawn characters and melodramas of *The Americans* aren't limited to the Soviet side. Elizabeth has made the brownies for their new neighbors, the family of Stan Beeman (Noah Emmerich), a genial guy who works for the FBI. Stan is assigned to the counterintelligence unit investigating the Soviet cell in the DC area—the very cell in which the Jenningses are based. So Stan is, at once, the series antagonist who threatens the very survival of the Jenningses, but also the American good guy in the spy-genre dynamic. Further complicating the moral complexity about espionage in this series, though, we see an FBI that's rife with deception, coercion, and violence, sometimes mirroring the brutal work of the Jenningses. In the first season, Stan commits a revenge murder and blackmails a Russian embassy worker, Nina Krilova (Annet Mahendru), whom he also seduces. Nor is he above some basic breaking and entering to snoop on the Jenningses. The pilot episode ends with Stan picking a lock to get into their garage because he's rightly suspicious about their car, where the kidnapping victim had been held. We see Stan check the trunk, now empty, and sneak out just as the camera reveals Philip hidden in the shadows, his gun drawn, ready to kill his friendly new neighbor.

Over the course of six seasons, the espionage narratives meld with the stories of marriage, friendship, and family. The FBI gradually closes in on the Soviet undercover network, while the Jenningses carry out heart-stopping operations literally under the noses of bureau agents and across the street from one of them. In the meantime, Philip and Stan develop a genuine friendship, while Stan's son becomes involved with the Jenningses' daughter, Paige. Stan's marriage breaks up, but the arranged marriage of Elizabeth and Philip develops into a real one as they fall in and out of love, separate, bond again, and then become bitterly and ideologically estranged. When Philip, in one of his alternate identities, legally marries FBI employee Martha Hanson (Alison Wright) in order to gain access to Stan's office,

FBI agent Stan Beeman (Noah Emmerich) and his wife, Sandra (Susan Misner), meet the Jenningses.

the metaphor of the Cold War as marriage makes a disturbing swivel. At one point, the Jenningses, their KGB handler, and Martha are all ensconced in a KGB safe house located in a middle-class DC neighborhood, where a dead rat infected with a bioweapon is stashed in the kitchen freezer ("The Rat" 4.6). It's a loaded metaphor of the horrifying incursion of state violence into domestic life.

In nearly every episode, suburban clichés and household details become charged with meaning, danger, and irony—doing laundry in the basement, getting home late from work, taking baked goods to new neighbors. When the Jenningses walk the brownies across the street to the Beemans, the two families awkwardly face each other as Stan announces where he works, and the camera focuses on Elizabeth's and Philip's faces as they absorb this blow and continue to smile. Later, Stan munches on one of the brownies and uses it to point across the street, telling his wife there's something "off" about Philip. It's unclear if Elizabeth escaped his eye because she's better at this, better at being ordinary, or because he's blinkered about gender, the first of his many mistakes in underestimating the women around him. The brownie in his hand is both perfectly innocuous and fraught with meaning, like that wobbly light fixture, the unremarkable material of everyday life when everyday life is the material of deception, surveillance, and secrecy.

Television and Cold War Histories

The seamless loop of espionage violence and family melodrama in *The Americans* revolutionized the television spy genre. Only ABC's *Alias* (2001–6) shared some similarities in that its protagonist, double-agent Sydney Bristow (Jennifer Garner), worked alongside her father in the CIA and eventually learned that her mother, presumed dead, is a Soviet spy. But Sydney's complicated relationships with her parents played out in the scenarios of espionage rather than the scenarios of the private home. The only previous spy series that included domestic scenes was *Scarecrow and Mrs. King* (CBS 1983–87), produced at the height of the Cold War, during the years represented on *The Americans*. *Charlie's Angels* alum Kate Jackson played Amanda King, the American housewife and single mother who was the unlikely partner and romantic interest of a seasoned male CIA agent. The title itself is a tip-off to the more conservative approach of this series. Unlike the upstairs-downstairs arrangement of *The Americans*, the family life of "Mrs. King" never overlapped with the espionage plots, and as Tricia Jenkins (2009) points out, the partnership worked along rigid gender lines; Amanda wasn't the one who delivered the fatal blows, and although she often struggled to balance work and motherhood, the series didn't question the gender politics shaping these problems.

The Americans also looked and sounded like no other television spy series and in fact owed more to cinema for its visual precedents. The showrunners say they were aiming for the look of offbeat investigation films like *Klute* (1971) and *All the President's Men* (1976), and they were at pains to avoid the more obvious tropes of film noir, like trench coats and shadowy alleys. The tense scenes are as likely to play out around a kitchen table as a city street (podcast 3.2). The fight and chase sequences, on the other hand, are straight out of 1980s buffed-up action films like the Rambo and Indiana Jones franchises, featuring elaborately choreographed pursuits, shoot-outs, hand-to-hand combat, and characters whose breathtaking martial arts skills are matched only by their speed and endurance. In the most striking influence from these films, Elizabeth is drawn as a kickass action heroine in the tradition of Ellen Ripley (Sigourney Weaver) from the 1980s *Alien* films, as described in the following chapter.

The painstaking re-creation of 1980s cars, homes, and clothing was enhanced by older optical techniques that reproduced the look of that era's photography and television. The colors are more muted and the images less crisp than what we see in contemporary television series. Cinematographer Richard Rutkowski aimed for a more "imperfect" look than what current digital technology delivers, so he supplemented the latter with 1980s equipment like an old zoom lens from that period. The result is a grainy look for both exterior shots and suburban living rooms. For night scenes on the street, the production crew relied on locations like the Gowanus neighborhood in Brooklyn, where older New York City streetlights hadn't yet been swapped out for LED lights that would have produced sharper images (Kreindler 2013; O'Falt 2017). This type of visual dimness is standard for noir crime stories, but in *The Americans*, the murky 1980s visual effects are attuned to a murkiness about history itself. Far from invoking nostalgia, the replication of the 1980s "look" invokes uncertainties about how, exactly, we should see Reagan's America and the Cold War.

This anti-nostalgia suffuses *The Americans*' use of 1980s rock music as well. Familiar hits are played in unfamiliar ways, like the explosive use of Fleetwood Mac's "The Chain" during a fast-action takedown of a South African Apartheid official on a busy street in season 3 ("Walter Taffet" 3.7). In the following season, Soft Cell's "Tainted Love" plays on a Walkman of a listener who can't hear Philip murdering someone behind him on a bus, while viewers hear the song mixed in with sounds of a man being choked to death.[7] At other times, the music links a thematic montage, as in the use of David Bowie's "Under Pressure" in an episode about Philip's torn allegiances toward both his wives as the FBI begins to target Martha. The erotic pulses of the song connect shots of Martha's lonely night in her bedroom, the lovemaking Elizabeth initiates with Philip, and the FBI surveillance team outside Martha's apartment ("Clark's Place" 4.5).

The thematic montages and dynamic editing make these sequences look like music videos, which came of age with MTV's debut in 1981, the year when the events of *The Americans'* first season take place, further knitting the series into cultural and television history. The songs used in *The Americans* aren't necessarily matched to the exact year of the series' events, but they were popular in this era. Early in the pilot, Philip and Elizabeth chase down and capture the Soviet defector to the distinctive percussion of Fleetwood Mac's "Tusk," its ominous drums feeding the tension of angry lyrics about paranoia and the end of love. The drumming in this song plays again in the pilot's final scene of Stan and Philip in the dark garage, and this time we again hear menacing lyrics keyed to the series' themes: "Why don't you tell me what's going on? / Why don't you tell me who's on the phone?" A similar match to theme is the use of Quarterflash's "Harden My Heart" in the opening scene of Elizabeth's seduction of the government official: "Darlin,' in your wildest dreams, you never had a clue."[8]

The pilot episode also features one of the standout music choices of the entire series, evoking a specific television history. Toward the end of that episode, when Elizabeth and Philip drive out to dispose of

---

7 Anna Varadi (2019) interprets this double playing of the song—the diegetic song on the Walkman and the non-diegetic mix—as a self-conscious exposure of the show's aesthetic reconstruction of the past as opposed to the "real" 1980s.

8 In interviews, *The Americans'* music directors P. J. Bloom and Amanda Krieg Thomas reveal the intricate planning that went into their collaborations with Weisberg and Fields, who were deeply invested in making the music significant. See Alston (2016) and Halperin (2018).

the defector's body and then make love in the car, we hear Phil Collins's husky, seductive "In the Air Tonight," with the song's lyrics carefully choreographed to the visuals. This scene marks the beginning of Elizabeth's emotional availability to Philip and her disclosure of her given Russian name in a subsequent scene, so there's a shot of her as we hear "I don't know if you know who I am." Moments later, we get a medium shot of the couple sitting silently in the car when the lyrics rise with the plaint cry, "It's all been a pack of lies."[9]

The entire sequence is a citation of the renowned use of this song in the 1984 pilot of *Miami Vice* (NBC 1984–90), the first television drama to use rock music as part of its soundtrack. The side-view close-ups of Philip and Elizabeth driving through the night and exchanging tense glances are identical to the shots of Detectives Sonny Crockett (Don Johnson) and Rico Tubbs (Philip Michael Thomas) driving at night to a dangerous operation. Given that the tension in *The Americans* scene is clearly sexual, the visual match to the earlier television drama suggests the repressed homoerotics of the slick Crockett-Tubbs coupling—a dynamic the *Miami Vice* sequence blatantly interrupts by having Crockett pull over to make an emotional phone call to his ex-wife, a reassuring detail for viewers after those looks he'd been getting from Tubbs.

But in *The Americans*' pilot episode, this mimicking of a famous sequence in a famous 1980s crime series mostly captures the vast differences between the two shows as representations of the 1980s, dramatizing changes in the television industry. *Miami Vice* had infused glamour and pastel fashions into its neo-noir narratives in which every crime was smugly resolved under brilliant Florida sunshine. Suave, unflappable Crockett and Tubbs were sometimes attracted to the dark side, but there's never any mistaking them for the bad guys.

9 See Alyssa Rosenberg (2013) on the meaning of the "In the Air Tonight" lyrics in relation to Elizabeth's revelation of the rape and revelation of her identity to Philip.

Shots of Elizabeth and Philip match those of Tubbs (Philip Michael Thomas) and Crockett (Don Johnson) in a famous sequence of the pilot of *Miami Vice* (NBC 1984–90).

In contrast, the "In the Air Tonight" reference in *The Americans* reminds us that only an entirely reconfigured television universe could feature compromised protagonists who collude in a murder in their garage and are bound together through "a pack of lies."

"A Must-Watch and a Hard Sell"

The Americans exemplifies the creative content made possible by niche marketing and narrowcasting (pitching to a specific audience) in the post-network era. This trend had enabled the popularity of violent antiheroes in series such as *The Sopranos* (HBO 1999–2007) and *Breaking Bad* (AMC 2008–13), the latter of which resembled *The Americans* as a cable-channel production that got rave reviews but only modest audiences—averaging 1.5 million viewers—for its first four seasons. But viewers doubled in numbers for *Breaking Bad*'s last season, and the numbers doubled again for the series finale, capturing ten million viewers, a number similar to the series finale of *The Sopranos*. By its final season, *Breaking Bad* had garnered drama awards, online buzz, and audiences who could catch up by bingeing on Netflix. The series shot from cult favorite to mainstream success.

FX hoped *The Americans*, highly acclaimed by critics, would forge the same path, given that its numbers similarly hovered around 1.5 million viewers for the first three seasons. But it attracted even fewer viewers in its final three seasons and didn't pick up a larger audience for its series finale. It was repeatedly snubbed by the Emmy Awards.[10] At the end of its third season, Salon critic Sonia Saraiya (2015) praised it as "The Best TV Show You're Not Watching," speculating

10 *The Americans* garnered eighteen Emmy nominations and won just four. It was nominated for Outstanding Drama Series only once, in 2018. Margo Martindale as KGB handler Claudia was the most successful, winning two of four nominations for Outstanding Guest Actress in a Drama Series. The other two awards went to Matthew Rhys for Best Actor in a Drama Series and to Joel Fields and Joe Weisberg for Outstanding Writing for a Drama Series, both in 2018.

that it alienated viewers who were asked to both sympathize with and keep a distance from the main characters. That was certainly the case for Tony Soprano and *Breaking Bad*'s Walter White, but Sairiya points out that unlike other series built around violent characters, *The Americans* offered neither humor nor hope, in addition to scenes spoken entirely in Russian. Emily Nussbaum (2015) of the *New Yorker* similarly warned viewers of the bleakness and heartbreak that haunt every episode, making it "at once a must-watch and a hard sell." This makes all the more significant the decision by the writers at the end of the first season, in the face of low ratings, "to actually lean harder into what made it great" even though it "would probably narrow its appeal" (Lynch 2018).

The stardom and casting of *The Americans* furthered the unsettling effects. Keri Russell and Mathew Rhys as antiheroes play shockingly against type. Russell started show business as a dancer on *The All-New Mickey Mouse Club* (Disney 1989–96), followed by an equally endearing role as the lead character in *Felicity* (WB 1998–2002), a series about a winsome college student. Viewers who knew Russell from her first gig were stunned to see her dance skills adapted to the choreography of vicious fight sequences. Welsh actor Matthew Rhys was likewise known for his television work as a sympathetic character, the gay lawyer on the melodrama *Brothers and Sisters* (ABC 2006–11). Also unnerving is the tough FBI counterintelligence director Frank Gaad being played by Richard Thomas, best known for his role as John-Boy on *The Waltons*, the CBS series that ran from 1972 to 1981, the year the action of *The Americans*' first season begins. The idyllic rural family life represented in *The Waltons* provides an especially ironic contrast with the troubled, secretive family life portrayed in *The Americans*.

The Americans fastidiously re-created the 1980s, with each script taking place on a specific date so that the fictional events could be coordinated with historical ones (podcast 4.1). But far from inviting nostalgia about the 1980s, *The Americans*' period details—from its chunky televisions to Phil Collins music and a grown-up John-Boy—aggressively ask us to reimagine that era in disquieting ways, beginning with the Reagan-era rhetoric linking family values to a strong America.[11] Along the same lines, the American perception of the Cold War itself comes under question as we see its key moments—Reagan's "Evil Empire" speech, the television screening of the antinuke melodrama *The Day After* (ABC 1983), Mikhail Gorbachev's initiation of glasnost and perestroika—from the other side. The series also invites us to reread Soviet and American history through the lenses of current politics. *The Americans* portrays the demoralizing effects of the Russians fighting a losing war in Afghanistan, for instance, painfully invoking the American war that had dragged on there since 2002. Viewers would have been especially aware of this during the 2014–15 rise of ISIS (the Islamic State of Iraq and Syria, as it was then commonly called), which resulted in the loss of Afghan cities such as Mosul that had been sites of earlier American victories. In addition, American-Russian relationships intensified with the election of Donald Trump in 2016, the fourth year of this series, so *The Americans*' narratives about Russian surveillance and American betrayals took on a new immediacy and added another level of perturbing implications about national loyalties.

Yet despite its outsider perspective and its critique of a nationalist "family values," *The Americans* is deeply rooted in Western ideologies that privilege private life and the pleasures of consumerism—that is, in Americanism. The series begins with an awakening that's emotional rather than political—Philip and Elizabeth stirred to passion—and it ends with their romantic commitment to endure. The grainy cinematography is offset by the lushness of "quality TV"—the slick music-video sequences, the choreographed action scenes, the R-rated sex

11 Reagan had invoked a return to traditional family values in his speech accepting his party's nomination for the presidency and continued to use the phrase and the sentiment in his rhetoric throughout his presidency, usually linking it to "shared values." The Ronald Reagan Presidential Library archive lists 1662 references to "family values" in Reagan's speeches and papers.

scenes, and the fine performances of its stars. But what makes *The Americans* significant in television and cultural history is its ongoing frictions with these pleasures, its relentless exposure of the contradictions of marriage, gender, family, nationalism, and the experience of "home."

The pleasure of melodrama itself revolves around these impossible contradictions and frictions, what Jonathan Goldberg calls melodrama's "productive impasses." The origins of the word itself—music ("melos") and drama—suggest the importance of elusiveness and ineffability in melodrama, he points out. Its emotional impact, like that of music, defies categories and polarities. Music "fills the air. It enters us," he writes, showing how melodrama similarly moves us toward empathy and feeling, and away from rigid identifications and the moral binaries described by Brooks (2016, 97). This perspective on melodrama helps account for our attachment to *The Americans*' KGB agents and also for the power of music in this series to bond us to its passion and violence.

Overview: Making It Real

This book follows the observation of showrunner Weisberg: "Everything that's successful in this show is about relationships" (podcast 5.1). So while much is to be written about history, seriality, narrative, and television aesthetics in *The Americans*, my focus here is the series' innovative uses of domestic melodrama and on melodrama's impossible scenarios. This focus also acknowledges the comment of Andrei Bezrukov, one of the Russian illegals arrested by the FBI in 2010, who said that while *The Americans* wasn't true to the uneventful nature of their work as spies, it was true to "the inner feelings" of their conflicted personal lives (Corera 2020, 310). The following chapters focus on the personal conflicts that invited viewers to empathize with the inner feelings of Cold War Soviet spies.

Chapter 1, "Wigs, Sex, and Women's Work," analyzes the portrayal of the series' extraordinary female characters who are involved with the KGB and who richly complicate generic portrayals of the female spy—Elizabeth Jennings, Nina Krilova, and KGB handler Claudia (Margo Martindale). These characters benefit from domestic melodrama's concern with women's suffering at the hand of institutions—in this case, the KGB and the FBI—and its sympathy for the woman who transgresses social norms and gendered power relations.

Chapter 2, "Marriage and Bromance," focuses on Philip's three primary relationships in this series—his two marriages and his deep friendship with Stan Beeman. While the Jenningses' marriage is the axis around which *The Americans* spins, Philip's lengthy and legal marriage to Martha provokes uneasy questions about what makes a marriage "real." Martha, the character who struck a nerve as the victim of Philip's cruelest espionage strategy, gets a lengthy analysis in this chapter, which also covers the series' much-discussed bromance between Philip and Stan.

This book concludes with a chapter on how Americanism and the American family are pictured on this series. "Family TV" argues that *The Americans*' most shocking and unprecedented tactic was the involvement of children in espionage. Paige and Henry (Keidrich Sellati) are conceived and born as collateral-damage risks, bound for orphanhood and the foster-care system if their parents are caught or killed. But the series also flips this concern by portraying adolescents who are themselves dangerous recruits in the KGB, including Paige herself. This chapter also pushes the question of what America and which Americans are pictured in this series and which are excluded or sidelined.

My attention to detail in these chapters is inspired by the talks with cast and crew available on the Slate podcast *The Americans*, hosted by June Thomas, which posted a discussion for each episode beginning with season 3. Interviews of the showrunners, writers, actors, directors, and production crew reveal their ardent commitment to political nuances, historical accuracy, character and theme development, and visual and audio aesthetics throughout the series. The writers quote Chekhov, the costume designers exclaim about finding a 1985 windbreaker, and the language adviser talks about coaching a Russian actor's dialect to match the character's class status. Each time I thought I might be reading too much into a scene or shot, I returned to the voices of these artists whose complex vision created a series that kept exceeding a singular interpretation.

1
WIGS, SEX, AND WOMEN'S WORK

The female spy in popular culture flickers between male fantasy and feminist figuration. She's very good at what she does, but much of what she does is women's work—seduction, glamour, masquerade. American Cold War children grew up with her animated cartoon version, the slinky Russian spy, Natasha, on *The Bullwinkle Show* (originally titled *Rocky and His Friends* [ABC/NBC 1959–63]), whose television history overlapped with that of the equally slinky British agent Emma Peel in *The Avengers* (ITV/ABC/Thames 1961–69). Diana Rigg as Peel performed the femme fatale with wit and style, as did her American counterpart who was the title character of *Honey West* (ABC 1965–66). At a time when women on television were housewives or nuns, these female spies were the outliers—skilled professionals in a male profession. Yet as Honey's name not so subtly suggests, no matter how quick they might be with a gun or a quip, their signature tools were cleavage and wigs.[1]

---

1 See Rosie White (2007) for a history of the cultural contradictions embodied in the spy genre's "violent femmes."

The Americans' timeline begins in 1981 when the wig-and-cleavage tropes for women spies were the only ones available in pop-culture history. Even *Scarecrow and Mrs. King*'s housewife-spy didn't appear until 1983. The sexy opening scene of *The Americans*' pilot episode delivers this cliché so seamlessly that only in retrospect do viewers realize they've been taken in as thoroughly as Elizabeth's hapless target. Wearing a Marilyn Monroe wig and low-cut cocktail dress, Elizabeth Jennings poses seductively on a bar stool, feigning awe when her mark brags about his Department of Justice job. Several shots frame her next to a mirror on the wall so we see both the character and her reflection, but even this visual cliché about female duplicity is complicated once the episode reveals that the themes of the entire series are double identities and the falseness of appearances. The platinum wig is a cliché but also a more nuanced emblem of the series itself.

Wigs are all about gender, and *The Americans* repeatedly plays up the implications of everyday gender performance in relation to character disguises and espionage. Philip often wears wigs, too, so the wig cliché transcends the female spy stereotype and instead symbolizes

The mirror on the left doubles the image of Elizabeth in a Marilyn Monroe wig, signaling the series' larger themes of double identities and false appearances.

the complexity of these characters whose jobs are deceit and impersonation.[2] For the women spies on *The Americans*, gender performance is central to their deceptions whether or not they're actually wearing disguises. The Jenningses' hard-nosed KGB handler Claudia is effective precisely because of her invisibility as a large older woman, and the reluctantly recruited spy Nina Krilova is effective because of her hypervisibility as a young, sexy one. In an additional twist on female role-playing, Elizabeth Jennings's disguises are not always about sex and seduction. Her performances of traditional femininity draw her into a real rather than fictional friendship as "Patty" in season 4, and she's forced into painful self-reflection while posing as a frumpy health-care worker in season 6.

As this suggests, the emotional core of this series resides in its aggrieved female characters, including Elizabeth and Philip's daughter, Paige, and Philip's other wife, Martha Hanson, both of whom are discussed in the following chapters. While Philip Jennings and Stan Beeman are engaging protagonists, their stories don't entail the same levels of complexity. Philip's fatherhood is never as conflicted as Elizabeth's motherhood, for instance, and his honey-trap entrapments don't involve the violence suffered by both Elizabeth and Nina. *The Americans*' deep emotional and narrative investment in these women stands in sharp contrast to other prestigious FX action dramas such as *The Shield* (2002–8), *Sons of Anarchy* (2008–14), and *Justified* (2010–15). As one critic put it, "The FX network has produced a critical darling that is not entirely awash in testosterone" (Borenstein 2016).

Jennings, Elizabeth

The Natasha cartoon is invoked as a joke by Elizabeth in a rare moment of relaxation with Paige in season 4. At this point, Paige knows

2 The *Atlantic*'s "Wig of the Week" feature affectionately called attention to the most "insane" wigs used weekly by both the Jenningses and commented on how the wigs sometimes allowed characters to express their "inner lives" (Zuckerman 2014b).

her parents are KGB agents, although she doesn't yet know that sex and violence are part of her mother's job. During a family bowling night, Paige asks her if the KGB taught her how to bowl. "Vital part of training," Elizabeth replies in a seductive, exaggerated Russian accent, and they both laugh gleefully ("Chloramphenicol" 4.4). Joe Weisberg said the script directs the line to be spoken "a la Natasha," mocking not just the femme-fatale prototype but also the bad Russian accents Americans heard on television all through the Cold War (podcast 4.4).

The Americans can joke about the Natasha caricature because Elizabeth's character derives from the more serious development of the female spy in twenty-first-century television, beginning with Sydney Bristow in *Alias*. *Alias* gave Sydney fabulous wigs and disguises but also gave her an in-depth personal life as a daughter, friend, and lover.[3] Similarly well-drawn women spies appeared in *Nikita* (CW 2010–13) and *Covert Affairs* (USA 2010–15). *The Americans* gives Elizabeth a rich emotional life and takes seriously her loneliness, her intimacies, and her homesickness. It also portrays her as the more politically astute of the two protagonists. She's attuned to American leftist interests through her relationship with Gregory (Derek Luke), a Black civil rights activist, and she has a meaningful friendship with Young Hee, a Korean immigrant, thus linking her to American minorities. She's the character we see most furiously reacting to Ronald Reagan's "Evil Empire" speech, and unlike Philip, she's unmoved by American materialism. "It's nicer here, yes. It's easier," she tells him. "It's not better" ("New Car" 2.8). Elizabeth remains the uncompromising communist even when the

3 Hagelin and Silverman point out that J. J. Abrams's inspiration for Sydney in *Alias* was reputedly the title character of his earlier series *Felicity*, which in turn had been Keri Russell's breakout role. *Felicity* suffered a public backlash and ratings drop when the character cut her long hair, suggesting the importance of traditional femininity in television heroines, Hagelin and Silverman argue, and adding resonance to Russell's performance of another heroine who defies feminine ideals (2022, 51–54).

Cold War is beginning to thaw through the diplomatic efforts initiated by Mikhail Gorbachev in 1985, which show up in the series' fifth season. Philip withdraws from the illegals program by the end of that season, but Elizabeth's change of heart comes very late in the series. When she does turn against the KGB hardliners, though, she exposes the Soviet operation and ends the entire espionage plot line.[4]

You can make a strong case that *The Americans* is Elizabeth Jennings's story. The series begins by prioritizing her perspective with the rape story, and her political trajectory mirrors the final years of the Cold War itself. Of the two protagonists, she's the one who changes the most. And perhaps most powerfully, *The Americans* centralizes Elizabeth in the series' most emotionally charged subplot, the Jenningses' involvement of teenage Paige in their espionage. If *The Americans* is Elizabeth's story, it's the story of a female anti-hero who transgresses ideologies of femininity not only in her uses of violence but in her violations of traditional motherhood, most egregiously in her disdain for the American coddling of children and her eagerness to recruit her daughter into the KGB.[5]

Elizabeth's motherhood, much more than Philip's fatherhood, animates much of the family melodrama in *The Americans*. Like Philip, she's a loving but somewhat distant parent to their younger child, Henry, who, as the least developed recurring character, comes off more as a prop for their American-family ensemble. But the Elizabeth-Paige

4 I am indebted to Allison McCracken, who pointed out the significance of Elizabeth's relationships with minority characters and also her affinity with 1980s action heroines. Allison's insights greatly enriched my reading of this character.

5 Sarah Hagelin and Gillian Silverman argue that unlike the male antihero, the female antihero is far more threatening because her abandonment of femininity poses a danger to the social fabric itself. Pointing out the primacy of motherhood in the characterization of Elizabeth, they describe how her recruitment of Paige into the KGB "deepens her cover" and profoundly threatens traditional ideologies of family and maternity because it "unmasks the way children may be owned and used in the service of the state" (2022, 68).

subplot seethes with the heat of maternal melodrama: mother-daughter conflict, boundary issues, fear of loss. In season 3, when Paige learns her parents' true identities and is revolted, Elizabeth is more visibly shaken than Philip. Philip fears that Paige will blow their cover by confiding in someone, but Elizabeth fears she's lost her daughter's love ("Stingers" 3.10). And after Paige tells the whole story to her spiritual adviser, Pastor Tim (Kelly AuCoin), Elizabeth is much harder on her than Philip is for putting the family in danger. Paige is forced to spy on the pastor to make certain he believes the Jenningses' pious story about how they're actually peace workers helping with human rights issues in El Salvador. When the teenager neglects her assignment just once, Elizabeth comes down on her full throttle about the urgency of both watching and performing for Pastor Tim: "Thanks to what you did, that's all that stands between us and this family being destroyed!" she shouts at her, while Paige quivers with tears ("The Magic of David Copperfield V" 4.8).

Paige believes her parents' sanitized version of their KGB work until she and her mother are attacked by a knife-wielding mugger late one night. Elizabeth easily overtakes him and cuts his throat with his own knife. Paige is shocked, suddenly realizing her mother has been trained for something more vicious than humanitarian aid work ("Dinner for Seven" 4.11). Elizabeth uses the opportunity to expound the feminist message that a well-trained KGB agent isn't as physically vulnerable as a woman. But soon she's teaching Paige martial arts in the basement, and we're seeing Paige becoming both empowered and indoctrinated. Exploiting Paige's idealism, she eventually recruits her daughter into the KGB's second-generation illegals program, against Philip's vehement protests.

The throat-slitting incident with the mugger and its consequence of Paige's recruitment encapsulate the thrills and perils of Elizabeth's power as a character. There's a lot of pleasure in having Paige—who can be a whiny teenager—see her mother spring into action as a fearsome avenger. She's finally seeing her mother for what we've always known her to be. And for female viewers, seeing Elizabeth's swift takedown of the mugger is a specifically *female* pleasure—the fantasy of confidence and safety, of walking dark streets without fear of assault. Elizabeth's physical prowess is a female pleasure throughout the series, in fact, perhaps culminating in her late-night sidewalk rumble with FBI director Gaad and one of his agents that leaves both men bloody and incapacitated. "A woman the size of my mother beat the crap out of me," the latter confesses abashedly to Stan, who generously responds, "I'm sure she could have taken down any one of us" ("Open House," 3.3). These incidents remind us that her character is indebted not only to Sydney Bristow but also to the action heroines of cinema that had become mainstreamed with the character Ripley in *Alien* (1979) and its 1980s sequels and with Sarah Connor in *The Terminator* (1984). Writing about the gender transgressions and the cultural disruptions of these "musculine" heroines, Yvonne Tasker (2002, 132–33, 151–52) reminds us that the threat of rape and the rape-revenge plot have always haunted this film tradition.[6] The revenge moment in *The Americans*' pilot episode—the ease with which Elizabeth kicks her rapist's head through the wall—is all the more significant as a confirmation of her self-sufficiency and the feminist implications of her character.

The problem is that Elizabeth's feminist dimensions—her competence, fierceness, and her purity in devotion to a cause—are complicated by scripting that makes her progressively more dogmatic, more violent, and less sympathetic than Philip, especially in the final season of the series. Her zealotry is evident when she uses the mugger incident to begin training Paige in self-defense, with lessons that become gradually more connected to training as a KGB operative. We grow suspicious of her motives when she does this, but we should also be suspicious of a narrative that punishes Elizabeth for her transgressions more than it punishes Philip—ultimately through the loss

6 My thanks to Brenda Weber for pointing out the importance of Elizabeth as a figure of female physical empowerment.

of Paige, which she'd feared most. The question is to what extent her character suffers disproportionately because she's an outlaw of both state and gender—the more dogmatically communist of the Jenningses and also the more outrageously transgressive because of her role as a mother. This suspicion of cultural bias needs to linger, but we also need to remember that melodrama itself sanctions and sympathizes with this kind of suffering. Kathleen Karlyn describes the key figure in domestic melodrama as the "excessive woman who desires too much," revolting against the rules of gender in which she's thoroughly imbricated as a wife, mother, daughter, lover (1995, 41).

The Americans breaks new ground by weaving Elizabeth's conflicts about these roles into her work as a driven patriot, willing to kill for her cause. In one of the most devastating scenes in the series, Elizabeth's identities as both daughter and mother unexpectedly implode when she has to kill an elderly woman who has become an unwitting witness ("Do Mail Robots Dream of Electric Sheep?" 3.9). During a break-in to a small shop, Elizabeth stumbles on the owner's mother, Betty (Lois Smith), who comes in at night to do the bookkeeping. The quiet nights at the office make her feel "in tune" with her deceased husband who'd started the business, she explains, and she talks about his service in World War II when he helped liberate Nazi concentration camps. Elizabeth is captivated by his GI photos on the desk, and we realize that she's thinking of her own father, who died in that war in 1942—in fact, shot as a deserter. Nevertheless, her mother and Betty had husbands who fought in a war when the United States and Russia were on the same side.

Elizabeth is so shaken by Betty's evocation of her mother, who's now seriously ill in Moscow, that she lets down her guard and, prompted by Betty's questions, reveals details of her personal life—her parents, husband, children, and even her name. Viewers sadly understand that she's making these disclosures because Betty can't survive as a witness. Instead of using physical violence, she has Betty overdose on her heart medicine, but this means Elizabeth must sit with her as she dies. Betty haltingly asks Elizabeth to explain why she's doing this, especially as a woman who has children of her own. When Elizabeth replies that she's doing it "to make the world a better place," Betty says, "That's what evil people tell themselves when they do evil things."

The word "evil" resonates because when Betty had talked about the GI photos, she'd mentioned the concentration camps, a knowable and external evil that had linked Betty's husband and Elizabeth's father as allies. But now Betty pointedly asks if killing her will make the world a better place. "Yes, it will," Elizabeth replies, but it rings hollow in the echo of Betty's quiet statement about evil. While Betty had spoken about feeling "in tune" with her husband, Elizabeth later hides her tears from Philip so he won't see that this killing has upset her. Elizabeth and Philip are sometimes deeply in tune with each other as espionage partners and spouses, but they are sometimes trapped in the silos of their own isolation and fears.

While Philip enjoys a true friendship with Stan, Elizabeth is singularly lonely. In heartbreaking subplots, we see her lose a man she'd loved and a woman whom she'd genuinely befriended. The relationship with the lover, the civil rights activist Gregory, had happened fifteen years previously, when her marriage was still an arrangement and Philip was still a stranger. She had recruited Gregory for work with the KGB and found someone she could finally talk with. "He was passionate about everything, passionate about me," she explains to Philip ("Gregory" 1.3). Years later, Gregory still loves her and makes the decision to die to protect her and Philip. The KGB plants evidence in Gregory's apartment to divert the feds from Philip, who'd killed an FBI agent. Claudia asks Gregory to do this as his "final act of service" for which he'll be protected by being safely exiled to Moscow. But realizing that a Black man in the USSR would face only a different version of racism, Gregory chooses suicide by cop instead, and we see him die in a gun battle on the street in a montage that also shows a dejected Elizabeth making a spaghetti dinner for her kids and catching television news of his death, all to the haunting music of Roberta

Flack's "To Love Somebody" ("Only You" 1.10). Gregory's loss is especially disheartening because he's one of *The Americans*' few uncompromised heroes, an idealist who decorates his apartment with Martin Luther King Jr. posters and believes socialism is the answer to American racism.

Another major loss for Elizabeth is that of her friend Young Hee (Ruthie Ann Miles) in a shattering season 4 story line about biological weapons. Disguised as "Patty" who sells Mary Kay cosmetics, Elizabeth manipulates a friendship with the charming housewife Young Hee to target the latter's husband, Don (Rob Yang), who has access to crucial medical codes about bioweapons. But the relationship between the two women develops into genuine affection. Elizabeth learns to cook Korean food, enjoys Young Hee's boisterous extended family, and laughs with her about cabbage dolls and Mary Kay rhetoric ("The Magic of David Copperfield V" 4.8). In *The Americans*' devious play of the real and the fictional, Young Hee shares stories of her family and background while "Patty" shares fake ones. All too real, though, is the damage Elizabeth inflicts when, to gain access to Don's files, Elizabeth

Elizabeth's former lover, civil rights activist Gregory Thomas (Derek Luke), chooses suicide by cop to save the Jenningses.

drugs him and tricks him into thinking he's seduced and impregnated her. A scuzzy version of Philip shows up at Don's office with news that his sister "Patty" has committed suicide, getting Don to leave the office so the KGB can do a sweep ("Dinner for Seven" 4.11). Elizabeth agonizes over this plan but agrees to it, and the friendship ends with a tearful Elizabeth listening to one last voice message from Young Hee, begging "Patty" to call because Don is acting so strangely. We realize Don will eventually tell his wife the whole sordid tale that may end their marriage.

In a series full of malicious stories, the Young Hee subplot stands out as especially punitive for both women. The twisted contrivances of the cover story, from Mary Kay cosmetics to pregnant "Patty's" suicide, are byzantine even for *The Americans*' convoluted espionage schemes. Why not just have the KGB break into Don's office? It's as if Elizabeth had to be exceptionally punished for carrying out this assignment and for betraying her friend "to make the world a better place," as she'd shakily told Betty. *The Americans* generally avoids this punishment of female ambition—especially remarkable given that the

In disguise as "Patty" with Young Hee (Ruthie Ann Miles), Elizabeth finds genuine friendship.

series takes place in the era of antifeminist backlash against the working woman who tries to "have it all."[7] Elizabeth deftly keeps a household going while she's working two jobs. She really is a travel agent, after all, and her other job involves sleepless nights and gruesome cleanup. And we actually see her selling Mary Kay cosmetics. The double bind of the ambitious woman is that she suffers terrible consequences because she's very good at what women aren't supposed to do. It's been a favorite theme of melodrama since the 1940s, when women in the workforce became a cultural issue, and characters like the heroine of *Mildred Pierce* (1945) learned that women could be successful at business or love but not both. A few years before *The Americans* debuted, *Mildred Pierce* was remade for television (HBO 2011), a spectral recurrence of the woman who is punished for not accepting that her life should focus on home, hearth, and heart.

And here's where the circuitry of domestic melodrama and espionage story tangle into a snare. Elizabeth as female antihero suffers the consequences of gender in ways that Philip's antiheroism does not. She and Philip both commit deceptive and violent acts, but by season 3 viewers perceived that Elizabeth's kill numbers were higher, according to online feedback (podcast 3.5). The viewer response suggests that no matter how fiercely Elizabeth is drawn as a kick-ass warrior, her character is still weighted down by the expectations of femininity. Her actions often have shock value because they violate feminine ideals of care, nurturing, and family. In the second season, she poses as a person in recovery in Alcoholics Anonymous so she can befriend and sponsor Lisa (Karen Pittman) who works at a plant that makes stealth aircraft ("Martial Eagle" 2.9). Elizabeth's AA pose abuses that organization's culture of trust and honesty, as well as its tradition that female bonding is important in the sponsorship relationship. Lisa is a mother of two small children, so her addiction is destroying an entire

7 See Esther Muñoz-González's (2018) discussion of the implications of Elizabeth as a working woman in the era of backlash against feminism.

family, making Elizabeth's fake sponsorship and lack of help all the more appalling. Things go very, very wrong. Lisa starts to drink again, and when she decides during a binge to confess her spying to the police, Elizabeth breaks a liquor bottle over her head and stabs her to death with the glass shards, an especially cruel ending for a woman struggling with alcoholism ("The Magic of David Copperfield V" 4.8).

At least Lisa's kids had been sent away to a relative's house so they wouldn't be the ones to find the body. That's not the case with the child of the Soviet couple Gennadi (Yuri Kolokolnikov) and Sofia (Darya Ekamasova), defectors protected by the FBI in season 6. Elizabeth slits their throats while their toddler is watching TV in the next room ("The Great Patriotic War" 6.5). Gennadi was supposed to be alone, and Philip could have made the same mistake and would have been similarly forced into the butchery of young parents. Instead this atrocity works as a dramatic strategy pushing Elizabeth's character to a place so dark that her redemption becomes increasingly urgent. But there's a suspiciously gendered bias about this strategy and about the nature of the darkness. The horror is not just that Elizabeth murders the parents but that Elizabeth *as a mother* could leave a small child to find his parents' bloody bodies.

She does it because she's a patriot and good soldier—but increasingly devoted to the wrong cause. Through most of the final season, which takes place in 1987, Elizabeth's character becomes harder and more dogmatic just as Gorbachev's rhetoric grows softer and he begins to implement reforms. She remains defiantly on the side of his hardline KGB opponents. "All this talk—perestroika and glasnost. The Americans eat it up," she complains bitterly to Philip. "They [Gorbachev's people] want us to be just like them. I don't want to be like them. And neither do the people back home." She tells him that every time she leaves the little enclave of Russian culture at the safe house, she's blindsided by the awfulness of America: "It hits me in the face. I hate it" ("Urban Transport Planning" 6.3). Further straining viewer sympathy in this episode, we see Elizabeth in the previous scene scrubbing blood off her face after killing an American military officer in a park. She's in front of a dirty mirror in a seedy public restroom, and the lenses of her fake eyeglasses have been splattered with blood. The restroom, the mirror, the glasses, Elizabeth's face—all of it is filthy. Blood has become her lens on the world.

In fact, through most of the final season, Elizabeth borders on monstrosity—the bloody face in the restroom mirror, the murder of Gennadi and Sofia, the seduction of a congressional intern who's not much older than her son ("The Summit" 6.8). One of her missions, an assignment in Chicago, is so botched that she has to call in Philip for help, even though he'd resigned from KGB assignments the previous year. The mission fails anyway, despite a high body count that includes a colleague's corpse they have to dismember with a fire ax in a parking garage ("Harvest" 6.7). And in a terrible allusion to the fake suicide of her fake Patty persona, her KGB colleagues give Elizabeth a very real cyanide pill that she wears around her neck like a macabre charm.

Finally, in the last episodes of the series, Elizabeth begins to doubt the KGB's plans to sabotage glasnost, leading to her decisions to kill a KGB saboteur and to expose the entire illegals program. Her turnaround begins with her assignment to gain access to a government official by posing as a health aide to his wife, Erica Haskard (Miriam Shor), a gifted artist in the final stage of a terminal illness ("Dead Hand" 6.1). Erica breaks through to Elizabeth, in the same way Betty had broken through in the repair-shop incident in the show's third season. This time, there's no motherly voice reprimanding her for evil but rather—even more relentlessly—a brilliant, dying artist demanding that Elizabeth do similar artwork so she can learn "how to see" ("The Great Patriotic War" 6.5). In constant pain and with little time left, Erica has no patience for any relationship that isn't meaningful, including her time with her health-care worker. Erica's drawings are stark self-portraits of a woman trapped within her agony, but lingering point-of-view shots suggest that Elizabeth sees them as portraits of herself as well. In the final minutes of the series finale, Erica's visions come to her in a dream as Elizabeth sleeps on the plane to Moscow. She dreams she's sleeping with Gregory in a room dominated by Erica's self-portrait, and on the table there's a portrait of Henry and Paige, obviously painted by Erica in the same style. They're images of the anguished losses Elizabeth has just suffered. Erica's self-reflection and self-portrait have become her own.

Elizabeth's turnaround develops from her own memories as well. In a flashback in one of the final episodes, we see the young cadet Elizabeth on her way to a KGB operation in Moscow, shrinking away from an accident victim on the street who's begging for help. Hoping she's done the right thing by refusing to be distracted from her mission, Elizabeth reports it to her female KGB instructor, who chides her for leaving a comrade in the street and warns her that she must keep her integrity while on assignment in America: "We do not want you to lose who you are" ("Jennings, Elizabeth" 6.9). In the previous episode, Philip had bluntly told her she'd lost herself, that she wasn't even human anymore—actually echoing a taunt that he himself had endured from a kidnap victim much earlier in the series. The implication is that Philip has become more human and Elizabeth less. These are the voices—Erica's, Philip's, the Moscow instructor's—that prompt Elizabeth to betray the KGB by preventing the assassination of a Soviet diplomat who's carrying Gorbachev's message to a summit in Washington. Killing the would-be assassin is Elizabeth's final murder for her country, but it's on behalf of the new Russia, Gorbachev's Russia, rather than the KGB. She then contacts Gorbachev's people and informs on Claudia's entire sleeper cell operation, effectively ending *The Americans'* story line of the Jenningses as illegals.

This episode is called "Jennings, Elizabeth," which is what Stan types into his FBI database to explore his suspicions about her. The title signals the theme of identity central to *The Americans*. "Jennings, Elizabeth" is the name that would have identified her if she were "in the system." She's not, of course, because "Jennings, Elizabeth" is a KGB fiction. It's also a chimera, the face on the FBI artist's sketches that Stan has been studying for years, refusing to see that it's his best friend's wife. But she's also barely recognizable in those sketches, and when Elizabeth makes the radical step of KGB betrayal, she is clarifying who she is—not only a patriot loyal to the new Soviet Union and capable of acting against the old one but also a woman who is true to her own conscience.

Elizabeth's act of redemption is far too late to save what really matters to her—her relationship with Paige. Even before Paige's decision to stay in the United States in the season finale, the mother-daughter relationship is shattered in one final blowup argument—ironically, about honey-trap sex, that sleazy cliché of female espionage work. It was the last truth about her life that she'd held back from Paige. Paige calls her a whore, and Elizabeth's furious response challenges the meanings, contexts, and value of sex: "It doesn't mean anything to me," Elizabeth roars. "I wasn't brought up like you. I had to fight every day. Sex? What was sex? Nobody cared, including your father." We've seen in flashbacks the grim postwar Moscow in which Philip and Elizabeth grew up, hungry and afraid. In a world of rubble and shortages, what was sex? Certainly it wasn't the bourgeois sex Paige learned about in her comfortable middle-class life in the suburbs. But Elizabeth's retort also glosses over the complicated ways she and Philip have responded to sex with others throughout their assignments as well as the importance of intimacy in their own relationship. Elizabeth had in fact coldly manipulated their sexual relationship earlier in season 6 to goad Philip into work for the KGB. So Elizabeth's angry argument suggests a deep defensiveness about the sex work that was a critical component of her espionage career. And it also returns us to the specter of Natasha and ultimately to how conventional femininity haunts the character of badass killer Elizabeth. This ambivalence stands as a significant contrast to the story of Nina, the other Natasha figure in *The Americans*.

Nina Krilova

Elizabeth outpaces the Natasha-style pop-culture female spy because her multiple story lines develop her character far beyond the stereotype. But Nina Krilova's more narrow role in this series at first slots her into the standard espionage trope—the glamorous and inscrutable femme fatale, untrained in espionage but expert in her use of sexual allure. Played by Russian-Indian actress Annet Mahendru, Nina is dark and slim like the Natasha cartoon, and she begins as a predictable plot device about male patriotism and bonding. She works in the Rezidentura, the center of KGB activity at the Russian embassy, and uses her position there for black-market trading so she can send money to her family in the USSR. The FBI is watchful for exactly this kind of culpable activity. Stan catches her in the act and blackmails her into becoming a mole so he can access insider information about the illegals program.

At first, this seems to be Stan's story more than Nina's. He falls in love, has an affair with her, and remains smitten even after she betrays him. At one point, he hands over a sensitive FBI file to the KGB in an effort to protect her. Even more seriously, when she's about to be sent to a Moscow prison because she fails to deliver on a KGB assignment, Stan comes close to committing treason by giving up defense plans in return for her safety. At the last minute, he can't do it, and he has to live with the part he plays in her imprisonment and eventual execution, even though he makes several attempts to save her. These attempts entail a tense truce with Nina's other lover, the likable Soviet embassy officer Oleg Burov (Costa Ronin). Nina becomes involved with Oleg after she's turned against Stan, and Oleg continues as a sympathetic character in the series long after Nina's death.

Stan and Oleg fail to save Nina, but it's the beginning of a beautiful friendship. Their relationship continues and resurfaces in the series' final season when Stan scrambles—unsuccessfully—to save Oleg from American counterintelligence forces. In male dramas like *Casablanca*

(1942), love triangles are obstinately focused on rival masculinities. The Ingrid Bergman character Ilsa may be captivating, but it's not her story, and she's swept unwillingly back into her marriage because the men in her life know better. On the surface, Nina's story structure is similar. "I had two lovers, one capitalist, one communist," Nina tells her cellmate in the Soviet Union. "I was whatever they wanted me to be. I loved them both, but in the end, they loved their countries more than they loved me" ("Born Again" 3.6).

Yet Nina's character exceeds this male fantasy of heroic men and a pliant, alluring woman. In a scene shortly after she agrees to work for Stan, she reports to him about getting information from her KGB boss, a plump, older man who lights up with lust every time she enters the room. When Stan asks how she got him to talk, she says, "I sucked his cock, just like you told me to" ("Comint" 1.5). Stan is genuinely shocked by this and protests that he never said such a thing, even though Nina's sex appeal would surely be her most valuable advantage as his mole at the Rezidentura. His surprise bluntly illustrates how sexism effectively works as oblivious indifference: it never occurred to him that Nina's bodily integrity would be involved in work on his behalf.

This happens in an episode that casts a harsh light on the exploitation of women's bodies for espionage. Elizabeth goes to bed with a target whose idea of foreplay is belt-whipping, and she plays the helpless woman—threatening to scream in the hotel room—rather than blow her cover. Later, she talks down an outraged Philip and insists that violence "happens sometimes" as part of the job and it doesn't matter. But the camera shows her bruised back, and we see her wince when Philip tries to touch the welts. Juxtaposed to Nina's bitter report of her own sex work, the incident pulls into focus the institutional abuse of women's bodies by both the KGB and the FBI. Elizabeth and Nina have far more partial-nudity scenes in this series than the men, and although these are staples of cable television with "adult content," they also suggest that women have a different kind of "skin in the game" when it comes to espionage.

Her KGB handler Claudia tells Elizabeth in this same episode that espionage is "twice as hard for women," and in the same conversation Claudia scoffs at American feminists who want the Equal Rights Amendment. Russian women know better, she says, than to rely on the law: "You can't wait for the laws to give you your rights. You have to take them, claim them, every second of every day, every month, every year." It's a surprising claim for a communist, implying that a socialist system that's supposed to provide for its citizens can't protect or provide for women, who have to "take" rights on their own. The institutional failure to protect women is evident in the joyless sex acts performed by both Elizabeth and Nina in this episode. Elizabeth at least has agreed to sex that "doesn't mean anything" as part of her job, but Nina is being blackmailed by the FBI for a crime that benefited only her family back in the Soviet Union.

Over the arc of her story line, Nina achieves a heroic stature that *The Americans* rarely confers on its characters. She makes two ethical decisions that put her in danger and eventually lead to her imprisonment and death. Because both of them involve treachery and the first involves sexual manipulation, her story doesn't immediately read like heroism and is haunted instead by the specter of the Natasha femme fatale. But in both decisions and turning points, Nina follows her conscience and resists the authorities who are pressuring her to take the easier route.

Her first major decision is to turn against Stan when she learns he's murdered an embassy friend of hers and then has lied to her about it. Furious, Nina confesses to the KGB her own treachery in exchange for information she can extract from Stan, continuing to be his lover but reporting all her activities back to the Rezidentura. "I serviced the subject orally before allowing him to penetrate me," she writes prosaically in one of her reports ("The Walk In" 2.3). So the later scenes of Nina's sexual performances with Stan are filtered through viewers' knowledge of her own alienation from these sex acts—her ability to summarize them in bureaucratic language—and also knowledge of her personal motivations and affection for the friend she lost at Stan's hands.

Nina Krilova (Annet Mahendru) appears to fit the stereotype of the slinky Russian spy but instead makes tough ethical decisions that give her character depth and compassion.

This gives Nina some personal agency against the bureaucratic pressures that have literally put her into bed with Stan. The FBI director gives Stan an apartment for his meetings with her, and while it's not explicitly spelled out, the assumption is that as long as they're lovers, Nina will continue to be a reliable source or, in the language of the FBI, an asset. On the part of the KGB, though, sex with Stan is explicitly spelled out in Nina's reports, accurately representing the way KGB agents were routinely instructed to use sex as necessary in covert operations.[8] Throughout *The Americans*, the KGB is consistently portrayed as more ruthless than the FBI, but the FBI's treatment of Nina is a prism through which we see how both institutions are linked in their apathy toward the use of women's bodies.

---

8 Joe Weisberg makes this observation about the routine use of sex by the KGB in the Slate podcast 4.6, commenting that the CIA—his former organization—would never have supported such a policy. It's especially interesting that in his scripts for *The Americans*, the FBI encourages Stan's affair less officially by supplying him with the apartment for his meetings with Nina.

After Stan refuses to betray his country for her, Nina is sent to a Moscow prison, where she risks an act of altruism that ends her life. At first she uses her skills at duplicity to benefit only herself. Promised a shorter sentence if she can coax a confession out of her Belgian cellmate, Nina gets the information she needs, showing her as a grimly pragmatic survivor ("Born Again" 3.6). Impressed, her jailers assign her to befriend and spy on the Russian scientist Anton Baklanov (Michael Aronov), a defector who had been kidnapped by the Jenningses in Washington, DC, and shipped back to the Soviet Union, where he's been forced to work on Soviet defense plans. Nina and Anton develop a genuine friendship that intensifies when she searches his rooms and finds loving letters to the son he'd left behind in the United States. This is the evidence she'd been instructed to find—proof that his heart and loyalty remain in the West with his child. But instead of reporting it, she tries smuggling one of his letters back to Washington to assure his son that his father still loves him. The letter is intercepted, and Nina is charged with a new crime that can mean only the death sentence.

Nina's final scenes are scripted entirely in Russian, subtitled in English, except for the occasions she and Anton speak English together as a way to have private conversations in Anton's lab. Weisberg and his cowriter, Fields, often remarked in the podcasts that their obsession with authenticity fueled their decision to have the Russian actors speak their own language. They also spoke about how the native language contributed to the "emotional authenticity" of the characters. The Russian journalist and activist Masha Gessen, who served as the translator for the last three seasons of the series, agreed and commented that Nina's character was especially enriched by Annet Mahendru's use of one of her native languages (podcast 4.6). In a *New Yorker* essay, Gessen (2018) remarked that *The Americans* was unique as a show "whose creators cared to insure that the dialogue was scripted and spoken in actual, idiomatic, living Russian." She also confirmed the writers' insight about emotional authenticity. Nina's character was "true," Gessen said, because she could articulate her sense of right and wrong in her Russian language.

Nina's execution is one of *The Americans* most shocking events. She's a sympathetic character spanning the first three and a half seasons of the series, and the script teased viewers with multiple routes of intervention and rescue through Oleg, Stan, and a husband she'd left behind in the Soviet Union many years before. We're even pulled into her escape fantasies during the last days of her imprisonment when she dreams that Stan has come to rescue her. But she wakes from one of those dreams to hear guards coming to get her for what they call a "transfer," and they march her to a nearly empty room where an official at a desk announces that her appeals have failed and she will be executed "shortly." Nina's legs buckle at this news, but even before viewers can fully comprehend the edict, a guard behind her pulls a gun and shoots her in the back of the head—a sentencing/execution strategy actually used in Soviet prisons because it was considered more humane than having the prisoner wait for an execution date (podcast 4.4).[9] In a long shot, we see Nina's body wrapped in burlap and removed. The officials continue their paperwork and pay no attention to the pool of blood in front of the desk. Only in retrospect do we realize that one of the few objects we saw in this room, as the

---

9 Weisberg pointed out in an interview (Hibberd 2016) that the staging of this scene followed the actual protocol of prison executions in the Soviet Union: "One of the most powerful things is that [historically the actual executions] were choreographed and staged by the execution team. Because they did it quite a number of times, they learned once the person heard what was going to happen to them, invariably their knees buckled. And so they learned to place a person on each side of them to catch them by their elbows, because they wanted to shoot the person in the back of the head—so they couldn't have the person fall. That was our staging, but also their staging. Also, the person read the verdict then stepped out of the way at the same time to not get blood on themselves. It was interesting to follow their actual staging, and to think about something like that being choreographed."

camera tracked her entrance, was a mop and bucket in a corner ("Chloramphenicol" 4.4).

Nina's dream sequences taunt viewers' beliefs in last-minute rescues as well as American optimism about justice and good intentions. Ironically, after all the treachery and double dealings of her past, Nina dies because she tried to connect a friend with his son. Her expendability offends our sense of fairness and reinforces *The Americans'* grim view that good intentions aren't necessarily rewarded or even necessarily good, as seen in the fervent patriotism of the KGB characters. But even though Nina's story line can't save her life, it saves this character from the clichés of the femme fatale and the male-bonding love triangle that otherwise stalk her narrative.

Claudia

While the ghost of Natasha haunts the story lines of Elizabeth and Nina, a more affable archetype hovers around the powerful woman who oversees much of the KGB action in *The Americans*. In a narrative littered with fake marriages and ersatz couples, the faux grandparent figures in *The Americans* are the people we know as Claudia and Gabriel (Frank Langella), the Jenningses' KGB handlers whose images as mild, kindly senior citizens belie their deadly power and Soviet authority. Claudia cooks an excellent *zharkoye*, a Russian stew, and watches Soviet movies with Paige and Elizabeth, exuding the warmth of a wise grandma. The KGB handler and her figurative granddaughter, Paige, are openly affectionate. But while Gabriel never breaks his benign demeanor, Claudia often unmasks to reveal a flinty Cold War combatant. She supervises a torture incident, murders a CIA officer, and antagonizes Elizabeth and Philip so aggressively in the first season that they put in a request to have her transferred back to Moscow. The request fails, and Margo Martindale goes on to play Claudia for the entire series, garnering four Emmy nominations and two wins for the role. "She is the best soldier of all," Martindale said about her character in an interview (Egner 2018) and on another occasion

Claudia (Margo Martindale) and Gabriel (Frank Langella) are the Jenningses' KGB handlers whose cover is their image as kindly senior citizens.

added that Claudia sees her younger self in Elizabeth, who is likewise "really a pretty brutal soldier" (Zuckerman 2014c).

Claudia continues *The Americans*' shrewd take on gender stereotypes in its portrayal of female spies. Claudia can openly walk around Washington, DC, doing the work of the KGB because her age, bulky size, and drab clothing make her invisible. She usually appears in a shapeless cloth coat, her hair permed and sprayed into matronly tidiness. Only the series' atmosphere of suspicion makes us think twice the first time we see her, drinking coffee in a sunny restaurant where Philip has stopped with Paige on a shopping trip. From the next table, Claudia catches bits of their conversation about how Elizabeth is likely to know about the verboten teen magazines Paige has purchased. "Maternal ESP," Claudia chimes in with a knowing chuckle, adding to Philip, "You have a lovely daughter." Paige beams ("Gregory" 1.3).

The scene brilliantly exploits the social nicety that a certain kind of public eavesdropping on child-parent interactions is okay. It's a way for adults to bond around the social contract about taking care of children. But then we see a shot of Philip watching her reflection on a silver water pitcher, and we realize this isn't an innocuous exchange. A few scenes later, he has Claudia by the throat in a dark alley, snarling "Don't you ever come near my kids again." She pushes him off and warns in return, "Don't you ever put your hands on me again"—though Philip isn't the one who eventually uses violence against her. The restaurant scene is all the more sinister in retrospect, given that Claudia's professional skill of eavesdropping on conversations merges flawlessly with her friendly senior-citizen persona.

When Philip tells Elizabeth about their new handler, he refers to her contemptuously as Granny, but in his first major encounter with her a few episodes later, Granny's in charge of torturing him because she suspects him of being a mole for the FBI—specifically, she suspects him of the leaks being facilitated by Nina ("Trust Me" 1.6). Beaten, waterboarded, and faced with the torture of Elizabeth as well, Philip refuses to crack, thus proving his loyalty, but Elizabeth turns on Claudia with fury, first attempting to drown her and then beating her savagely around the face. Both these women are veteran KGB agents, but it's nonetheless unsettling to see the fit, athletic Elizabeth beating up Granny and leaving her as a bloodied mess on the concrete floor. "Tell whoever approved this that your face is a present from me to them. Show them your face! Show it to them!" Elizabeth screams. Her cry sums up *The Americans*' steely tension about how bodies and faces can express and disguise truth and identity, especially given the twist ending to this incident: Philip and Elizabeth deliberately crash their car into a tree so they have a plausible excuse when their children see their bruised, swollen faces, undercutting Elizabeth's cry that a bloody face can convey the truth.

Claudia's singular killing on *The Americans* is an act of personal revenge, making it all the more chilling as a revelation of Granny's deadly skills ("The Colonel" 1.13). In a curly gray wig and pastel-framed glasses, embodying a dotty old lady who's locked herself out of her apartment, she manages to get inside the apartment of a vigilant CIA director who hides a pistol in his belt when he answers the door. But within seconds, Claudia has tasered him, slit his throat, and injected a paralysis drug so that in the ten minutes it will take him to bleed out, as she tells him, he'll be forced to listen to her explanation of why he's being murdered to avenge his own recent murder of a KGB officer. Claudia could have killed him instantly, but this CIA officer needs to hear her story while he dies.

And we need to hear the story, too, as a reminder of Claudia's thirty-five-year history as a Russian soldier and patriot. She's avenging the death of General Vijktor Zhukov (Olek Krupa), she explains, whom she'd known since the Russian defeat of the Nazis in 1945. His loss is personal because, as we'd learned in a previous episode, Zhukov was her lover in those days. It's the only reference to a romantic relationship we ever get about Claudia. Later in the series, she and Gabriel operate like an elderly couple together, but there's no hint they ever had a connection outside of their work. So the one romance in Claudia's backstory is linked to a key moment in Soviet history. As she calmly tells the dying CIA officer, she met Zhukov at the battle of Stalingrad when he had two dead Nazis at his feet.

Claudia's only other backstory is likewise linked to the war against the Nazis and dramatizes the power of this history for a certain generation of Cold War hardliners. *The Americans* offers glimpses of gloomy postwar Moscow through flashbacks to the Jenningses' impoverished childhoods, but Claudia's is the generation that experienced the war itself and internalized its lessons about stoicism and loyalty to the USSR. During an intense history lesson for Paige in the series' final season, Claudia explains that Russians don't refer to the war as "World War II" but instead call it "the Great Patriotic War"—not a global battle but a national one, beginning with the 1941 Nazi invasion and ending with the Red Army push that finally defeated Germany. The United States lost four hundred thousand troops in that war, Claudia tells Paige, but Russia lost twenty-seven million people, including civilians. Claudia points to a photo of a shelled-out building in a history book. "I was here," she says, "and my youngest brother was killed there," adding that she lost her entire family during the Battle of Stalingrad. It's the only time in the series in which we hear Claudia's voice tremor with emotion ("The Great Patriotic War" 6.5).

Claudia's pinpointing of herself in the history book photo, an invisible victim in a much larger conflict, suggests her unfortunate place in Cold War history as well. Soviet nationalism is her whole life, so she's the character most clearly doomed by *The Americans*' historical narrative. When Elizabeth sabotages the KGB plot against Gorbachev's perestroika and exposes Claudia's operation, Elizabeth has slipped into the winning side of history, and Claudia remains on the other. In their grim final encounter at Claudia's apartment ("Jennings, Elizabeth" 6.9), Claudia has just made some *ukha*, a Russian fish soup, which she offers Elizabeth, who turns it down in a classic gesture of rejection/rebellion against the maternal figure. Claudia is staggered by Elizabeth's news of her takedown of the entire operation, and she expresses her disappointment in terms of her wartime past. "You always reminded me of the women I fought with in the war, the way you

Claudia shows Paige (Holly Taylor) a photo of the Moscow building where she lost her family in the Great Patriotic War, which Americans call World War II.

put country over self," she says, "but now I see you never understood what you were fighting for." Claudia says she'll go back home to engage in the new internal war for the real Soviet Union, now threatened by Gorbachev's liberals: "I'm not afraid. We took it back from our enemies once before, we'll do it again." When Elizabeth leaves, Claudia stays at the table and continues eating her *ukha*. The last we see of the most powerful female spy in *The Americans* is a tough, determined older woman stubbornly enjoying her Russian soup.

2
MARRIAGE AND BROMANCE

Elizabeth Jennings's betrayal of the KGB is a dramatic turning point of *The Americans*, but it's not the series climax. The climax instead is Stan Beeman's betrayal of the FBI. Having finally identified, tracked, and trapped the illegals he'd been pursuing for the entire series, Stan holds Elizabeth, Philip, and Paige at gunpoint in a parking garage, just yards from their getaway car, in the series finale. When he orders them to lie down per FBI protocol for making his arrests, they refuse. "This is Paige!" Elizabeth cries, invoking his affection for the entire family. But this scene belongs to Philip and Stan, who engage in a heated reckoning of how much of their relationship was real and how much was deceit. "You were my only friend in my whole shitty life," Philip tells him. Stan's anger is tangible, but so is his hurt. "I would have done anything for you, Philip, for all of you," he says. Philip talks him down, appealing to their common ground as fathers, friends, and patriots doing their jobs. And Stan lets them go. Later, we see him lie about it to his FBI colleague, and the last we see of him, he's grimly supervising the feds as they dismantle the Jenningses' home across from his own, coming to terms with his betrayal of job and country. He had refused to commit treason for his lover Nina. But he's done it for the love of his friend.

Stan, heartbroken, listens to Philip describe the tangle of lies and genuine feeling that made up their friendship.

The Americans' showrunners and reviewers often talked about marriage as a metaphor for the Cold War in this series, with the Jenningses enacting edgy stalemates and messy compromises. But this final twist takes the conflict metaphor in a different direction. Faced with a life-or-death confrontation, Stan is persuaded that the only good solution is for everyone to walk away. The consequences otherwise would be devastating, as recognized in bitter Cold War standoffs like the 1953 Korean armistice, the 1960 U-2 spy plane interception, and the 1962 Cuban missile crisis. The Philip-Stan friendship was similarly a high-stakes gamble that depended on Philip's identity remaining a secret. Otherwise, each would kill the other if necessary. We saw this deadly zero-sum calculation in the pilot episode, which ends with Philip hiding in the shadows of his garage, pointing a gun at Stan, who's broken in to check out his suspicion about a car used in a kidnapping. The series has come full circle and ended with the men again in a garage, with the pointed gun in Stan's hand this time. The truth about the Jenningses is out in the open, but also "out" at this point is the depth of Stan's friendship with Philip.[1] The fate of the Jennings family—Do they get caught? How does their Cold War end?—comes down to bromance, not marriage.

This chapter begins with a focus on Philip as the linchpin in the marriage and bromance story lines. He's the linchpin in this series' other marriage story as well. In his Clark Westerfeld persona, he's legally married to Martha Hanson, who is Stan's secretary at the FBI. All three relationships—with Elizabeth, Martha, and Stan—start as arrangements and grow into something authentic, elaborating *The Americans*' explorations of what's "real." The Jenningses are assigned to each other in a fake marriage, but they fall in love and eventually even have a Russian Orthodox marriage ceremony. Philip starts playing racquetball with Stan so he can keep tabs on the enemy, but soon they're sharing beers and empathizing about their marital problems and then about Philip's failing travel business. And while Philip marries Martha only to get access to Stan's office—surely the most loathsome of these arrangements—he gradually cares enough about her to defy KGB orders so he can save her life. Marriage predominates as *The Americans*' central dynamic, but bromance animates the same themes of loyalty, betrayal, vulnerability, and remorse.

Bromance was the term widely used by reviewers and by the writers themselves. And although we see the dynamic also play out with Nina's two lovers, Stan and Oleg, the relationship between Stan and Philip colored the entire series. "There's no question about it," commented showrunner Joe Weisberg, "through all the layers of bulls— and lying and manipulation and everything else, it's hard to argue that these two men didn't love each other" (Friedlander 2018). At one point Elizabeth teases Philip about a misunderstanding that's led Stan to think Philip is involved with Stan's estranged wife. "Make up with

1 In her close reading of the scene in the garage, Angelica Jade Bastién (2018) describes the performance of "raw, nerved vulnerability" by both Matthew Rhys and Noah Emmerich and the shot compositions focusing on the emotional tolls on their faces and bodies.

your boyfriend yet?" she asks ("Pastor Tim" 4.2). Stan's suspicion of Philip about an affair instead of espionage doesn't bode well for Stan's spy instincts. We see this misdirected suspicion again in the final season, when Stan's instincts tell him "something is going on" because Philip is clearly stressed out—actually about Elizabeth's botched assignment in Chicago that has pulled him back into KGB activity. Deeply worried about his friend, Stan confronts him in an emotional conversation in which Philip confesses ("I didn't want to tell you . . .") not to what's going on in the espionage business but to the failure of the travel business—which is in fact actually going on as well. Philip is so moved by Stan's compassion that he initiates a long hug with his friend, which we see in a close-up as heartbreaking as those of his embraces of Martha ("Harvest" 6.7).

In some ways, Stan and Martha are equally blinkered by love. For six seasons, Stan stares at the police-artist sketch of his friend without recognizing him. At times, the irony edges into Kafka-esque absurdity. At the end of season 1, Stan is involved in an FBI car chase and shoot-out, not knowing his friends the Jenningses are in the car he's pursuing. He's among the shooters in the bloody melee when Elizabeth is hit and seriously wounded. That evening, as she recovers at a KGB safe house, Philip phones Stan to ask if he'd please go across the street and check on the kids. The absurdity would be comical except for the series' underlying premise about how deeply deception may lurk in relationships with those we love best.

The term *bromance* has been circulating in pop culture since 2005 to describe buddy films and male-duo television series featuring emotional intimacy between straight men—Starsky and Hutch, Butch and Sundance, Judd Apatow's nerd movies—and high-profile celebrity friendships like Matt Damon / Ben Affleck, Brad Pitt / George Clooney, Barack Obama / Jay Z. The term signaled a growing perception about sexuality as a porous boundary rather than a bulletproof identity. Bromance is a way to both acknowledge this and laugh it off, per the MTV series *Bromance* (2008–9) and the 2009 film *I Love You, Man*. As Michael

DeAngelis writes, the entire concept is based on awareness of what's not there; the men have an intense bond but won't "take it to the next level" (2014, 1–2). The fascination of the relationship is this risk, and the dynamic is disavowal of the very possibility: "I know very well, but all the same . . ." (3). In *The Americans*, a flashback reveals that Philip has had sex with at least one man as part of his KGB training in how to fake sexual desire and "make it real" ("Salang Pass" 3.5). But queer desire isn't the vibe or the tension in his relationship with Stan. The risk and denial is about espionage rather than sex. The high-stakes secret is that Philip can "make it real" only by sharing the truth of who he is, shattering the friendship and endangering his entire family.

How to "make it real"—KGB spies posing as a suburban couple—is *The Americans*' central riddle, elusive and unsolvable because its marriages and bromances endlessly shift the very meaning of "realness." The Philip-Stan friendship exemplifies this conundrum and shows how the tensions around authenticity are ideological as well. The relationship with Stan allows Philip to explore his "real" feelings in ways that he can't do with Elizabeth, specifically in the EST (Erhard Seminars Training) program that Stan coaxes him into. The EST movement, which later morphed into the Forum, was a group-therapy enterprise of the 1980s that promised self-transformation through ruthless honesty about a past or current situation. The concept taps profoundly American ideologies of self-help and individual enlightenment, so it's ironic that Stan is the one who gives up on it, while Philip is intrigued and stays. EST haunts Philip's entire story line in *The Americans*, given his series-long struggle to make an honest appraisal of the malicious work he does for the KGB. He sums it up in his explanation to Stan in that final confrontation in the garage: "I did all this stuff, Stan, I don't even know why anymore. It seemed like the right thing to do for my country. . . . I kept doing it, telling myself it was important, until finally I couldn't. And I stopped." In the plea for himself and his family, Philip's final pitch to Stan is about what he learned in the group therapy sessions: "I wish you'd stayed with me at EST. You might know what to do here." But Stan does know what to do, suggesting that the moral weight of *The Americans* lies more with the emotional individualism characterizing EST than with political ideology and patriotism. That is, it lies with the more ineffable dynamic of melodrama, to use Goldberg's (2016) terms.

Given its self-help Americanism and the promise of seeing your life in a new way, EST is a line in the sand for Elizabeth, who's already alarmed by Philip's inclination to see himself as an American—someone who wears cowboy boots and buys himself a Camaro Z/28. Elizabeth attends an EST session to find out what Philip likes about it, and she concedes its value in talking about "difficult things." But her final take is that it's one more "very American" con job, pushing people to buy more sessions. Philip sees the tapping of "real" emotion, but Elizabeth sees the tapping of wallets. The argument escalates quickly into a row about past infidelities, and suddenly Philip and Elizabeth are screaming at each other, obviously unable to deal with "difficult things" ("Magic of David Copperfield V" 4.8). EST also figures in Elizabeth's most contemptuous reproach to Philip in the final season, when they're no longer on the same side of the Cold War. He's withdrawn from work for the KGB and has refused to send an innocent young woman into a dangerous situation overseas, as Elizabeth had asked him to do. They're barely speaking to each other, and Philip tells her they need to talk because "it's better not to let bad feelings fester." Furious, she crudely links EST and bromance erotics, retorting, "You can take your Forum bullshit and you can shove it up your ass" ("Rififi" 6.6).

Philip's openness toward his own feelings and toward American culture makes him the more relatable of the Jennings couple, as described by multiple reviewers and by the actors as well, in discussing how they interpreted their roles (Prudom 2013; Sandberg 2015a, 2015b). In addition to his heartfelt friendship with Stan, Philip relates to their kids better than Elizabeth does. In the season 1 finale, when they argue about which of them will go on a high-risk assignment that could leave the other one as a single parent, Elizabeth insists she should go because the kids like Philip better. She wins that argument. And the more emotional pitch of Philip's character ultimately saves himself and his family. The climactic face-off with Stan isn't a shootout or physical struggle but an argument as plaintive and sad as a lovers' quarrel, riven with hurt and regret.

Making Philip the "softer" of the communist couple reverses traditional gender expectations, but gender works in far more traditional ways in making him a more palatable character than Elizabeth. Both the Jenningses are murderous antiheroes, but following a long television tradition of that violent character type, Philip can still come across as the likable one in a way that Elizabeth cannot. Men aren't as centrally identified with their family roles, so viewers have long been okay with Tony Soprano or with *Breaking Bad*'s Walter White being enmeshed in disquieting contradictions about marriage, family, and children. Their masculinity isn't at stake, the way femininity is at stake in picturing a female antihero like Elizabeth. Philip's most despicable behaviors are never at odds with masculine stereotypes about violence, promiscuity, and predatory sexual behavior—the bad behaviors for which men routinely get a pass.

He's a loving and protective father to his teenage daughter, Paige, for instance, but in his grubby Jim persona, he sleeps with Kimmy (Julia Garner), a young woman of the same age, to gain her trust. Arguably, he redeems himself because Kimmy is the one he refuses to exploit for the high-risk assignment in season 6, enraging Elizabeth about his emotional "bullshit." But sex with a smitten college student lurks in his troubling history. Likewise, he loves his son, Henry, but we learn that he was Henry's age when he killed for the first time; his victim was another young boy in Moscow who'd been bullying him ("Glanders" 4.1). Masculine stereotypes plague the scripts about his marriage and infidelities too. His love for Elizabeth is unshakable, but that doesn't prevent him from a tender weekend in bed with Irina, the woman he'd loved as a young man in Moscow. And most controversially, Philip courts and marries Martha, then uses toxic ploys to get her to turn against her bosses at the FBI.

Marriage: Philip and Elizabeth, Clark and Martha

What can you say about a marriage best captured in an incident involving amateur dentistry? In one of the series' most viscerally disturbing scenes, Philip uses pliers to pull out one of Elizabeth's teeth because she can't risk going to a dentist who might report a mouth injury she incurred in her sidewalk fight with FBI agents. When the FBI goes after the mystery woman, she barely escapes a multiple-car pursuit and returns home badly shaken. Philip enfolds her tenderly in his arms, but when he tries to kiss her, she flinches from the pain in her mouth. He takes her by the hand and leads her gently down to the basement garage where we see he's laid out the pliers and a bottle of bourbon—the anesthetic—on a table. In an unrelenting four minutes, we get one of the most excruciating scenes of the entire series. Tight close-ups focus on Elizabeth's widening eyes and Philip's shadowed face as he bends toward her. "Oh god," she whispers before they begin, and then there's no dialogue, just her occasional whimper and rapid breathing. After several twists of his hand, Philip pulls something out of her mouth, and the ordeal seems to be over, but he shakes his head: it's only a fragment of the tooth. He has to go in and try again. She at first closes her hand around his hand on the pliers as if to stop him, but then she braces herself with her hands on his chest and opens her mouth even wider ("Open House" 3.3).

It's a sex scene. Elizabeth's grasp of the pliers was consent. We're watching him probe inside her, and we're caught in the middle of their intense wide gazes as the camera alternates extreme close-ups of their eyes. *The Americans* includes several explicit sex scenes between the Jenningses, but in no other is the camera placed into such close proximity—literally in their faces—through the entire experience. Her eyes on Philip show dread for the pain but even more than that, total faith in him. She trusts him entirely. Unlike the Cold War, this is no metaphor for their marriage. It *is* their marriage—harrowing, perverse, sometimes almost unbearable to watch. The Jenningses' painful marital crises provoke the same mix of fascination and horror—the recruitment of their daughter into the KGB, Philip's lengthy marriage to Martha, their estrangement as Philip retreats from the illegals' operation while Elizabeth becomes its most vicious assassin.

The Jenningses' marriage is the ground zero of espionage in this series, the structure that allows the KGB to operate the illegals' program in suburbia. It's also the emotional through line, as suspenseful as any of the KGB operations. The series begins when Philip and Elizabeth begin to fall in love, fourteen years into the KGB arrangement in the illegals program. Their new relationship is immediately imperiled by infidelities. Elizabeth's bond to her ex-lover Gregory ends with his death, but Philip's brief liaison with his former lover Irina, from his youth in Moscow, nearly ends the marriage. By the end of season 1, Philip is living in a one-star motel where Stan brings him six-packs and glum camaraderie. The motel is a wistful allusion to the Jenningses' newlywed motel scene glimpsed in the pilot episode when they learn about window air conditioners and a nervous Elizabeth tells her new husband she's not ready to sleep with him. Now, sex with his former lover has driven Elizabeth to throw him out of the house. She could have lived with this unfaithfulness in the days when she and Philip were KGB partners in a fake marriage. She herself had sought love and solace with Gregory. But she's deeply hurt now that her relationship with Philip has become emotional and—in the logic of the series—real.

Questions of loyalty, betrayal, and "realness" in *The Americans* crisscross and bind together the marriage and espionage stories. For more than half the series, as part of his KGB assignment, Philip is legally married to Martha under the name Clark Westerfeld, sporting a floppy wig characterized by the *Atlantic*'s "Wig of the Week" report as "supremely sleazy" (Zuckerman 2014a). It's a "real" marriage in that he's not committing bigamy, having never married Elizabeth, and although it's illegal to use a false name in a marriage application, it doesn't invalidate the marriage. Their church wedding, where Elizabeth poses as Clark's sister, Jennifer, is especially tense because it happens during the time Philip and Elizabeth are separated ("The Oath" 1.12). We see Philip later in the episode pleasuring Martha on their wedding night, a sex act officially blessed by the church and state but also—for viewers invested in his relationship with Elizabeth—a marital sex scene that's disconcerting precisely because of its legitimacy. The conflicting "realness" of the overlapping marriages—Clark and Martha, Philip and Elizabeth—inflames the marital melodrama of *The Americans* and impels its uncomfortable questions about the meanings of marriage.

When the Jenningses reconcile and are at home together at the start of season 2, Clark's ongoing marriage to Martha plays an even sharper contrapuntal role. Elizabeth's curiosity and uneasiness about Philip's other marriage leads to a loathsome sex scene. Posing again as Philip's sister, Elizabeth coaxes some tipsy girl talk out of Martha and

For more than half the series, Philip is legally married to Martha Hanson (Alison Wright) in his disguise as Clark Westerfeld.

is unnerved to hear that Clark, although a "gentleman" in every other way, is "wild . . . an animal" in bed where, Martha says meaningfully, "he makes me his" ("The Deal" 2.5). The camera focuses on Elizabeth's changing face as she hears this. Shortly afterward, Elizabeth seduces Philip just as he arrives home from Martha's place and playfully insists he keep his Clark disguise on, glasses and all. "I want Clark," she says, and is disappointed when he starts to go down on her because, she complains, "It's the same." When Philip is exasperated by this, Elizabeth explains, "She said he was an animal." Suddenly Martha is in the bedroom with Clark and Elizabeth, the two marriages unnervingly scrambled ("Behind the Red Door" 2.6).

But even more unnerving is the question of what's "the same." The sex? The husband? Earlier, when Elizabeth made a comment about Martha as his "wife," Philip sullenly objected: "She's not my wife." Now, furious with her demands for a different husband, Philip roughly forces himself on Elizabeth and leaves her crying on the bed. In the bathroom, he glares at himself in the mirror as he angrily tugs at his wig, and when he fails to disentangle it, the hairy mess slides to the side of his face, so the mirror shows a monstrous man who's just sexually assaulted his wife. Elizabeth sobs with pain and humiliation, and Philip glowers at himself in the mirror because the atrocity extends beyond the violent sex: they'd wanted to pretend that Clark and Philip are two different people with different wives and sex lives and instead had to acknowledge that they're "the same."

Martha's threat to the Jenningses' marriage sharpens once she's targeted by the FBI and becomes a fugitive, hidden away in the safe house with her fake/real husband, her ersatz sister-in-law, and KGB handler Gabriel, the grandfatherly patriarch of this bizarre family. Gabriel, downstairs in the living room, can hear Martha and Philip making love in one of the upstairs bedrooms. Gabriel had wanted to drop Martha and leave her to the FBI once she'd become a risk to the operation, but in a vehement argument, Philip demanded they protect her and get her exfiltrated to the USSR.

Still, Gabriel tells the Jenningses that they may "have no choice" about what to do if Martha makes a scene in public. So the tension ratchets up when Martha makes a run for it and Elizabeth finds her in a city park, in a wide-open area where the FBI are also looking for her. As she approaches, viewers see Elizabeth's hand ominously in her jacket pocket where there is surely a knife or gun. She pulls Martha into a strong embrace, and Martha gasps. Viewers gasped too. But Elizabeth has only sucker-punched her, and as she supports the stunned Martha with both arms and leads her away, they look like grieving sisters or friends or lovers, poignantly reminding us of the physical intimacy they share with Philip. Elizabeth had "no choice" about using violence, and given the public place, she also had no choice about how fatal the blow could be. Yet unmistakably it's a blow on behalf of her marriage and her jealousy. Her husband is showing a devotion and concern for Martha that's not in the job description.

Back at the safe house, a subdued Elizabeth asks Philip if he wants to go back to the USSR with Martha and "just get out of this whole

Elizabeth has just sucker-punched Martha, but they look like grieving sisters or lovers, a reminder of the intimacy they share through Philip.

life," adding sadly, "I'd understand." Surprised, Philip denies he would want such a thing. "I love you," he insists, but viewers realize—and Elizabeth realizes—it's a statement he's made to Martha too ("Travel Agents" 4.7). In the previous episode, "The Rat," he'd already shocked Gabriel and Elizabeth by revealing that he'd shed the Clark wig and glasses as a way to win Martha's trust. "Martha's seen me," Philip says simply, and fans can hear the echo of Elizabeth's scream to Claudia, "Show them your face!" from season 1. "Did you *want* her to *see* you?" Elizabeth asks incredulously. In espionage, being "seen" means being discovered and revealed. It means giving up the advantage.

What exactly has Martha seen that alarms Elizabeth? There's no evidence that Philip is in love with Martha, but he's fond of her, is touched by her plight, and is haunted with guilt about what he's done to her. This is the episode named for a dead rat that's infected with a fatal bioweapon and that's stashed in the kitchen freezer, and it's difficult not to think of Philip as the same reprehensible creature. But Martha has also seen his emotional accessibility and honesty, verboten traits for a KGB agent working an asset. Nursing the bruise from Elizabeth's punch, Martha asks him outright what his real name is, and he tells her not only his American name but also his Russian name. "Mikhail," he tells her, "but everyone called me Mischa." The fake name, the real name, the familiar nickname—Philip has unraveled three layers of identity to her, a dramatic turn in a marriage based on deception. Only Elizabeth knows all these identities. Little wonder she's threatened.

Elizabeth advises Philip to tell Martha he'll come along with her to the USSR or join her there later in order to make it easier to get her on the plane. But Philip doesn't do that, demonstrating his deep respect for Martha and also his trust that she'll be strong enough to accept the truth of her lonely exile. He's right. Martha is calm and dignified in her final scenes on American soil. The only lie Philip maintains is about his relationship with Elizabeth. He flat out denies he's sleeping with her, shielding Martha from his nastiest betrayal. If there was any doubt about Philip's emotional bond with her, the only time we see him cry in this series is when he puts Martha on the plane the following morning before dawn, in a scene so grim and silent that it looks like she's being marched off to execution ("Travel Agents" 4.7). In fact, Nina's execution occurred only a few episodes previously, so viewers are acutely aware of what can happen when a woman gets involved in espionage not of her own choosing.

Marriage: "The Martha"

Martha was the only character on *The Americans* who sparked her own Twitter following. Her #poormartha followers worried and speculated about her fate through the first four seasons of the series and cheered when she made cameo appearances in the fifth. But the character got plenty of online trolling, too, and some reviewers dismissed the Martha plot as farcical or as "cringe-inducing comedy."[2] It's a different kind of cringe from the ones evoked by the absurdities around the Stan-Philip friendship. Paradoxically, even though Stan doesn't know the "real" Philip, he does know a Philip who is real—the thoughtful friend, the good father, the dependable neighbor. Stan isn't actively gulled like Martha, who blinks away every red flag about the fictitious Clark. Clark tells her that because he's an internal investigator for the FBI, the marriage must remain a secret at her workplace. Also, he says his job requires him to spend most nights away from her and to keep his own apartment. Most of all, he needs her help making sure the FBI office is secure, and she can do this by secretly photocopying classified files.

As outrageous as it may seem, the Martha operation is based on an actual Cold War KGB strategy called the Secretary Offensive, used in West Germany in the decades after World War II. According to KGB

2 Jessica Goldstein (2016) uses this phrase to describe early responses to Martha. Also see Gazelle Amami's (2016) interview with Wright alluding to the reviewers who first saw Martha as "comic relief."

documents smuggled out of Moscow by a prominent defector, agents from East Germany targeted women who worked in important government offices and had access to classified documents. The agents were dubbed "Romeo spies," and they aimed for long-term commitment: "Love, or a plausible semblance of it, was capable of generating more intelligence over a longer period than brief sexual encounters." The agents had their greatest success with "lonely female secretaries, most in their thirties or forties."[3] Martha Hanson fits the bill. The pilot script describes her as "very plain," making her especially vulnerable to Philip's charms as the smarmy Clark. Martha successfully smuggles documents home in her purse, but her most dangerous feat, bugging the director's office with a microphone pen, nosedives when the bug is discovered, triggering an urgent FBI internal investigation and Martha's agonized suspicions. "Who are you, Clark?" she asks tearfully when his cover starts to fall apart. "I'm your husband, the man you married, who loves you more than you can ever know," Philip replies earnestly ("Divestment" 3.8). Poor Martha!

This exchange about knowledge and love resounds paradoxically as we gradually see that Philip is more emotionally attached to her than *he* could ever know. But the cruelty of this exchange also reflects a larger narrative cruelty about Martha. Viewers always know more than Martha knows, and though that's true of Stan as well, Stan as an FBI officer has other kinds of narrative power and agency. Martha does not. More than that, viewers are situated to think of Elizabeth, not Martha, as Philip's "real" wife despite the status of the Jenningses' marriage as a KGB fiction. So every time Philip says, "I'm your husband"—as he does often, as a way of assuring Martha of his commitment to her—viewers

3 Showrunners Joe Weisberg and Joel Fields claim they relied on this source, the Vasili Mitrokhin archive, for details of KGB operations. Christopher Andrew and Vasili Mitrokhin describe several secretaries' operations and the suicides of some of the women involved (1999, 445–50.) The Secretary Offensive was unique to the KGB, but a similar tactic was used in the 1980s by UK intelligence forces to infiltrate protest groups (see Collins 2014).

are cued to remember that he's *really* the husband of Elizabeth and also that Elizabeth is far more savvy. When Martha agrees to Philip's condition that they can't live together once they're married, we know Elizabeth would never have been conned like this. Also, Elizabeth can take on various roles and multiple looks, from glamorous to dowdy, as part of her arsenal of disguises and roles. But Martha's choices are few and are directly tied to what she looks like, the "very plain" thirty-something secretary suddenly wooed by an ardent suitor.

Martha's fans empathized with the story of an innocent woman beguiled by love, but many critics dismissed her as a "sad sack" and "patsy." And once she became a liability, hunted by the FBI, "Martha death watches" showed up online, characterizing her as "someone most fans of *The Americans* were eager to see killed off" (Zuckerman 2014a; Lyons 2013; Rowles 2016; Robinson 2017a). But as the FBI closed in, Martha was mostly a danger to herself. Worrisome props appeared. She had a gun in her purse and also a vial of pills. When she wandered to the railing of a high bridge, viewers were surely being pushed to imagine—or secretly hope for—a suicide that would solve everyone's problems.

The polarized viewer reactions to Martha's character—empathizing with her or wishing her dead—suggest she touched a nerve. The nerve might be her sheer ordinariness, distinct from the glossiness of *The Americans*' main characters. She's more like us than like the Jenningses or Beemans, and her everyday decency shakes up viewer complicity with the Jenningses' murderous behavior. Hers is the face—plain, unremarkable—that registers Philip/Clark's moral vileness in the episode where he tells her he's killed her office colleague Gene (Luke Robertson) to protect her. Close-ups show her palpable horror as she backs away from him, terrified and then doubly stricken as she realizes her own involvement. "What have you done? What have *I* done?" ("Glanders" 4.1). Her cries could well reflect viewer discomfort with our empathy for the Jenningses. Martha knows only about Gene. We know much more.

Martha also strikes a nerve with anyone who's been romantically duped, from cheated partners to victims of online dating scams. We're all capable of not seeing clearly the people we love, like Stan staring at the artist's sketch of his best friend: "I know very well, but all the same . . ." Philip in fact fears that Stan might be the victim of a KGB honey-trap scheme when Stan takes up with a woman who's a little too inquisitive about his work. "I don't want Stan to be like Martha," Philip frets ("Darkroom" 5.10). But Martha emerges from a specifically female tradition, the Gothic film and fiction heroines who ask the desperate question "Whom have I married?" When Philip slowly peels off his wig for Martha to reveal the person she's "really" wedded, it's a scene from a horror movie, the unmasking of the monster ("I Am Abassin Zadran" 3.12). Most of our own stories about suspicion and repressed knowledge are less dramatic. Alison Wright remarked in numerous interviews that Martha's gullibility reflects common stories of people in denial about their relationships. Far from being the exception, Martha is "what all of us would most likely be in this scenario," Wright commented. "We'd like to think that we'd be the Jennings[es]—that we'd be bad-asses. But the likelihood is that we'd be the Martha" (Robinson 2017b).

Gender biases make it easier to blame "the Martha" rather than blame Philip's bad behavior, even though Philip is at his most despicable in this operation. Wright herself pinpointed this dynamic, characterizing online criticism about Martha as "the typical let's blame the woman: How could she be so stupid? How could she not realize? . . . that's very much akin to, you know: What was she wearing? How short was her skirt? Was she really asking for it? Did she deserve it?" (Scott 2017). Her character is also built around the gender biases about the female bodies that usually inhabit spy dramas. "I didn't think that people who looked like me could be on TV," Wright commented in an interview about her career (Heller 2017)—which has in fact demonstrated that her looks can be dialed down but also glammed up, as seen in her characters on *Feud: Bette and Joan* (FX 2017) and *Sneaky Pete* (Amazon 2015–19). Wright believed that audience responses to her character fell out along gender lines. In personal encounters while she was filming the show, she said, women usually told her Martha was their favorite character, while men usually commented that she was better looking in person than on the series (podcast 4.6), an indirect comment on what kind of female bodies "could be on TV."

In spy dramas, women are far more likely to look like "the Nina," who's legible as a slinky femme fatale. But "the Martha" is more confounding. The showrunners pointed out that Martha is "constantly surprising you with her wisdom, her sense of humor, her overwhelming dignity" (Heller 2017). I would add to that list her joyful, robust sexuality, which is also unusual for television women scripted as "very plain." In sex scenes with Philip/Clark, Martha is consistently the more eager, vocal, and aggressive partner. She has condoms at the ready, and she's radiant in her flimsy lingerie. She's the sexier one in these scenes as well, because Philip/Clark is often pictured in a mildly funny light. For one thing, he refuses to take off his glasses for sex. "I can't see a thing," he explains, but it's far more likely he needs to cling to a disguise in order to participate in this chicanery. In one episode, Martha's on top of him, but he can't perform because she's wearing a necklace that Elizabeth begrudgingly handed over to him to use as a gift, and the necklace is waving in his face ("Mutually Assured Destruction" 1.8). Philip is especially comical in a shot in which he's anxiously checking Martha's copy of the *Kama Sutra* as he struggles to maintain a precarious position ("EST Men" 3.1). Later, when Martha has become a suspect and Stan searches her apartment, Stan finds the *Kama Sutra* and stops at that same dog-eared page, regarding it with a puzzlement that is television's puzzlement about the healthy sexuality of women designated as "plain" ("Chloramphenicol" 4.4).

Stan's surprise is reflected by that of his colleague Aderholt, who's been assigned to take Martha on a dinner date while Stan conducts the search. In a parallel-edited scene, while Stan is learning about Martha's

In their sex scenes, Martha is joyful and lusty, while Philip/Clark, who refuses to take off his glasses, is mildly comical.

sex life, Aderholt asks her if she's seeing someone, and Martha lies to him with a coolness that would make the Jenningses proud, telling him she's in a relationship with a married man—perhaps a clue that she knows, on some subconscious level, what "Clark" won't admit about his "sister." "We're discreet but I'm not wearing wigs and sneaking into hotel rooms," she says—surely a snipe at the wigs we've seen throughout the series but also referring to the fact that it's Philip, not herself, who wears the dreadful wig as Clark. In an episode long before Clark allows Martha to "see" him, she remarks casually to him that she knows he wears a toupee, stunning both Philip and viewers ("Operation Chronicle" 2.12). It's a moment of comedy, but it's also clear that we've all been underestimating her, as evident in Aderholt's barely contained shock as he listens to Martha calmly talking about adultery.

The showrunners claimed that in the writers' room, Martha was always considered "sexy" (podcast 4.7), but those writers created scenes and conversations in which Martha's looks are discussed in a way that other female characters' looks are not. The most disturbing of these is the doctored-tape incident after Martha has planted the microphone in Gaad's office. The tape catches Gaad in a conversation saying, "Martha's not so bad"—clearly part of a rowdy, male-bonding bull session that he sanctimoniously interrupts: "All right, men, Martha's a good girl," he says primly. "Leave her alone" ("New Car" 2.8). In one of Philip's more ghastly acts in the series, he edits the tape to make it sound far worse, in an effort to alienate Martha from her colleagues. In the version he plays for Martha, she hears Gaad and his colleagues seem to talk about her as an "ugly old lady" incapable of sex appeal: "Ten Scotches and a bag over her head before I'd touch her." It makes her cry. And it works. "Better that I know who they really are," she says morosely, a line that stings because the people she doesn't "really" know are her fake in-laws and her fake husband who has just played her a partly fake but humiliating recording to coerce her into some dangerous work ("Martial Eagle" 2.9). And here's where the narrative cruelty links Martha's looks and Martha's lack of knowledge. She's up against more glamorous people who are positioned to outsmart her. When Philip asks Elizabeth to listen to the doctored tape, we see her turn away, appalled, but she agrees that it would work.

The final conversation about Martha's looks occurs after Martha has become a suspect and after Stan has found the *Kama Sutra*. At the FBI office the next day, Stan does some digging on Martha and shares with Aderholt that she'd had an abortion as a teenager in 1964, when it was still illegal. Stan is making the point that Martha is capable of breaking the law, but that's not the question he poses to Aderholt: "Do you find Martha attractive?" he asks. Stan is confounded not just by Martha's ability to do espionage work under his nose but also by her ability to have a healthy sexuality under those drab office clothes. And he connects these two kinds of secrets. Aderholt replies that "there's something sexy about her." I would argue that the "something" explains Martha's appeal to many women viewers—sexiness not attached to a traditionally glamorous female body. The "something" is also what eludes Stan, who consistently underestimates the women around him—Nina, Elizabeth, and even his wife, Sandra, who mocks him for being the counterintelligence guy who doesn't see she's having an affair. In season 2, he has a dream connecting Martha's duplicity as a spy to the sexual duplicity of his wife. In the dream, Martha is stealing files and directing him to Gaad's office where he finds his wife having sex with another man ("Echo" 2.13). Stan can't process what his subconscious is telling him about female smarts and sexuality.

But while *The Americans* taunts viewers with some mean narrative tactics about Martha, it also grants her the narrative coup of successfully outfoxing the FBI. When Stan and Gaad realize that Martha has been in a secret marriage to a KGB operative and has been doing undercover work under their noses, it's a triumph for Team Martha and a sly reversal of the Martha subplot. The FBI, after all, has been in the dark even longer than she has. As a *New York Times* reviewer commented about Gaad's stunned reaction, "Has any character outside of a comedy ever been as pathetically, permanently sucker-punched as Agent Gaad?" (Hale 2016). The comedy echoes that of Martha's casual revelation that she knows about the wig: this is what happens when you underestimate Martha.

The women involved in the KGB Secretary Offensive often took their own lives once they discovered they'd committed treason and had married men who were only pretending to love them. But that's not Martha's fate, nor does she meet the kind of violent end that happens with Nina, the other woman sexually exploited by state espionage in this series. That's because unlike Nina, who's deserted by Stan, Martha is championed by Philip. The writers give him a line that may express their own estimation of Martha when he tells her tenderly, "You are one of the most true and honest and good women I have ever known" ("Divestment" 3.8). It makes her victimization by Philip all the more heinous.

Martha's Twitter feed lit up when, several episodes after her removal to the USSR, she's glimpsed in the background at a sparsely stocked Moscow grocery store, picking through the canned goods, wearing a shapeless coat and paisley babushka, in a scene about another character ("The Midges" 5.3). The shock is that she's faded into an inconspicuous background figure, part of the collective proletariat. Fans were happier a few episodes later, when Gabriel visits her Moscow apartment and she refuses his offers of comfort or friendship, silently going back to cooking potatoes. Her Twitter followers applauded her for brushing him off. And in her final scene, her KGB language tutor has taken her to a playground where the children, he tells her, are orphans. There's a little girl who starts to bond with her. "She's all alone," the tutor tells Martha, implying that the two of them need each other and that an adoption could be possible. Earlier, during her marriage to Clark, Martha had tried to persuade him to foster a child, and in one of Philip's more repugnant moves, he plays along with her for a while to maintain her trust. But now her dream of becoming a mother is possible even if her dream of love with Clark has been obliterated. "We want you to be happy," the KGB tutor tells her, and Martha's fans heard those words as their own.

Marriage: Elizabeth and Philip, Nadezhda and Mikhail

The Martha crisis, combined with Philip's use of EST as a way to cope with it, leaves Philip and Elizabeth alienated and hostile at the end of season 4, to the point that Gabriel, alarmed at their exhausted despair, gives them some time off from operations so they can heal. And they do. By the following season, they've become so close as a couple that when they're assigned dual honey-trap operations in the Midwest, they balk ("What's the Matter with Kansas?" 5.4). Matthew Rhys commented that the Jenningses "become more and more married" once the marriage with Martha is over (podcast 5.4). Assigned to seduce and sleep with people in Kansas, they resist Gabriel's orders. "It's not a good time for us," Elizabeth says vaguely, sounding like someone scrambling for an excuse to duck a family reunion. But they're responsible agents, so they dutifully pack their disguises and head to the wheat fields, where the KGB believes the United States has a plot to starve the Soviet Union by shipping them a defective wheat hybrid.

The assignment is a disaster. Only after the Jenningses have killed an innocent lab worker do they learn that the US government grain experiment, far from being a genocide plan, is an attempt to crossbreed a wheat plant that resists disease. But even in their remorse about the lab worker, the Jenningses are united. Elizabeth offers to do missions on her own, given Philip's growing unease with work for the KGB. But he insists they're together in this: "No, no. It's us, Elizabeth. It's us" ("Lotus 1-2-3" 5.5).

Given this deep bond, it's not surprising that they marry each other in a Russian Orthodox wedding ceremony in the middle of season 5. It's Philip's idea. He takes Elizabeth to a dark warehouse where Father Andrei (Konstantin Lavysh), a Russian Orthodox priest, is waiting with the wedding liturgy and rings. "It's not perfect," Philip whispers to Elizabeth about the religious framework—"God and all," he apologizes ("Darkroom" 5.10). The scene is spoken entirely in Russian, and they use their real names, Nadezhda and Mikhail. They had driven there wearing fake oversize glasses, but they've removed them, showing their faces to God and all. This is Philip's second wedding in this series, the first one being the one with Martha, which had been entirely legitimate. So it's especially important that this one, even if "not perfect" and not legal, is rendered genuine through their names, their language, their faces without disguise. Keri Russell commented that the wedding is the Jenningses' "little electric secret" to keep from the KGB, a way to claim something of their own that the authorities don't know about (podcast 5.10). The secret used to be that they were not actually married, but now the secret is that indeed they are.

A few episodes later, a much sadder bonding gives them a scary glimpse of what they might become. They're assigned to assassinate an older woman in Massachusetts who was a wartime Nazi collaborator—or at least is suspected to be. "I can't just get this order from them and do whatever they say," Philip says, revealing his growing reluctance about work as an illegal ("Dyatkovo" 5.11). When they track down the collaborator, they find she's a suburban grandmother

Philip arranges a traditional Russian Orthodox wedding so that he and Elizabeth are married in the church as Mikhail and Nadezhda.

with a poignant story about having been sixteen years old when the Nazis killed her parents and forced her into unspeakable acts against her own countrymen. She'd kept this secret even from her husband, who listens in sorrow and horror to her confession. Close-ups of Philip and Elizabeth show them deeply troubled not only by her story but also by its unsettling familiarity, surely imagining someone tracking them down, decades in the future, holding them accountable for their violent pasts: "It's us, Elizabeth. It's us." So when Elizabeth shoots both the woman and her husband, it looks more like personal anger and frustration rather than an execution on behalf of the homeland. In the car afterward, Elizabeth suddenly tells Philip: "I want to get out of here. We should just go. I mean it. Let's go home." But it's Philip who, disillusioned, withdraws from KGB activities by the end of season 5, disclosing the Jenningses' emotional and ideological estrangement that's in full-scale escalation by the beginning of season 6.

At the start of that final season, the Jenningses' marriage is crumbling, and so is the USSR. Philip and Elizabeth aren't even on the same side anymore. The always-lurking questions about realness and authenticity rear up because they each believe they're working for the "real" Soviet Union. Philip is approached by Oleg, Nina's former lover who had returned to Moscow but is back in the United States without diplomatic status. He's been sent by former Rezidentura chief Arkady Zotov (Lev Gorn), now a private Moscow citizen hoping to stop the KGB's campaign against Gorbachev ("Dead Hand" 6.1). But Oleg reveals that Gorbachev's power is so limited that he can't even remove the hardliners who are trying to take him down. Elizabeth is working for those hardliners, and Philip agrees to make reports on what she's doing.

So the Cold War itself is no longer the spy-versus-spy story from *The Americans*' earlier seasons. Once Philip agrees to spy on Elizabeth for Oleg, that dynamic takes on a whole new meaning. The larger Soviet political scene represented in *The Americans* is also conflicted. In the series finale, Arkady advises Oleg's father in Moscow that both of them are now targets of the KGB. Contemporary television viewers know the history gets even murkier. The USSR was indeed disassembled over the following years but lingered so strongly in national nostalgia that it was easy for former KGB officer Vladimir Putin to reassemble a totalitarian state not even a generation later—not exactly the "real" USSR but also not exactly an alternative.

To what extent does *The Americans* similarly undermine the concept of a "real" marriage, especially in light of the emotional depth scripted for the Clark-Martha marriage and the troubling persistence of its arc over four of the series' six seasons? *The Americans*' most radical premise is that identities and relationships are scripts and performances. Enacting the roles of an American suburban couple, the Jenningses do in fact become one, with multiple television sets and private-school tuition bills for Henry. Is marriage, like national identity, a matter of performance and habit as well? In the melancholy "make it real" episode, Philip explains to Elizabeth that he's been trained by the KGB how to perform passion, and that's how he can "make it real" with Martha. The kicker is his confession that he's "sometimes" done it with Elizabeth, too, an uneasy reminder that the KBG ploy echoes the everyday experience of long-term relationships ("Salang Pass" 3.5). Similarly, when Philip/Clark repeatedly tells Martha, "I'm your husband," it may be a strategy straight out of the Secretary Offensive playbook, but Elizabeth grows alarmed as he begins to act that way, too, in the final days before Martha's exile. The authenticity of the Clark-Martha marriage—its legal standing, the church wedding, Martha's joyous wifehood, Philip's growing sense of responsibility toward her—is profoundly troubling, given what we know about its context. From the inside, from Martha's side, where the scripts insistently take us, it feels real.

But the Jenningses' marriage is the emotional hook of *The Americans*, and the discomfort of watching Philip's marriage to Martha is that viewers are set up to root for the Jenningses as the "real" marriage of the series. The Russian Orthodox wedding not only cements this claim but also symbolically ends the marriage to Martha. Philip's use of his real name, Mikhail, vanquishes the fictional Clark. Even the structuring of the series around the Jenningses' marriage as a saga, wrought with crises and periods of alienation, offers a version of what a "real" marriage may feel like. There's a second, symbolic wedding, too, during the series finale, in a nighttime scene deep in a forest where Philip, Elizabeth, and Paige stop to bury their identification cards and passports. Philip and Elizabeth throw their wedding rings into the hole in the ground too. The Jenningses, even as a KGB fiction, are no more. But the burial is a wedding as well. Along with their wigs and new identity papers, Elizabeth hands out two new wedding rings, which she and Philip slip on, silently, above the hole in the dark, frozen woods. They may be the rings they used with Father Andrei, who at that very moment is being forced to give them up to the FBI, admitting he saw them once without their disguises. Viewers know it was the day of the wedding in the warehouse. His betrayal is the final twist in the braided marriage-espionage stories, which have finally brought Philip and Elizabeth on the same side again, fleeing to their homeland.

Will it become their "real" home, the way their KGB assignment made them, to some extent, real Americans—the suburbs, the TVs, the Camaro Z/28? And is this the version of America that *The Americans* offers as "real," through the Jenningses as a 1980s television family? These are the issues explored in the following chapter on the Cold War family and the America represented in this series.

3
FAMILY TV

Cold War Television

When the Statue of Liberty disappears during season 4 of *The Americans*, the action pauses, and the Jenningses watch, fascinated, as magician David Copperfield performs a feat seen nationwide in a television special that aired April 8, 1983.[1] The four Jenningses gathered together watching 1980s television look like a 1980s television family—white, heterosexual, attractive, comfortably middle class, in a house where there's not just a living room but a family TV room—American media centrism built into the architecture itself. Copperfield appears to make the Statue of Liberty vanish and then rematerialize, and the Jenningses are entranced by the stunt's sheer audacity and spectacle. Copperfield's event was good TV.

1 *The Magic of David Copperfield V*, in which the magician makes the Statue of Liberty "disappear," was the fifth of a series of eighteen Copperfield specials between 1977 and 2001. The statue seemed to disappear because Copperfield tilted the platform on which the audience and camera were positioned. Brenda Weber points out how this shift of perspective encapsulates *The Americans*' tilting of its audience's relationship to the Cold War (personal correspondence, May 2021).

Looking like a 1980s TV family, the Jenningses watch David Copperfield make the Statue of Liberty disappear in a television special. Pictured here are Philip, Elizabeth, Paige, and Henry (Keidrich Sellati).

At this point in *The Americans*, the Cold War is being fought at ground level through unhappy marriages, children, and lovers. Philip and Elizabeth are quarrelsome and exhausted after Martha's exile. Their daughter, Paige, is still profoundly shaken by the news that her parents are Soviet agents. At the FBI, the Martha scandal has resulted in the firing of Director Gaad, whose parting advice to Stan is that he's letting his guilt about Nina impede his work. And Stan's divorce papers have just come through, evidence of how the detritus of the Nina subplot has washed into his personal life as well. Given the series' focus on marriage and the suburban family to tell stories of Cold War espionage, the question is how *The Americans* weaves together these stories and genres in picturing the Cold War and also in picturing Americans—a question implicit in the series' title about an identity that's assigned and performed by its protagonists.

The episode featuring the Copperfield stunt suggests the importance of television itself in this complicated representation of history, national identity, and the American family. In its larger project, *The*

Americans demonstrates how we inevitably understand this history—or any historical conflict—through popular culture. The amalgamation of fiction and history is evident in the title of this episode, "The Magic of David Copperfield V: The Statue of Liberty Disappears" (4.8), which was also the title of the 1983 television special. The same is true of a later episode about the national broadcast of the antinuke film *The Day After* (4.9). The other meta-television episode, "March 8, 1983" (3.13) is named for the date of Ronald Reagan's much-heralded "Evil Empire" speech, a high point of tension in both the Cold War and the Jenningses' family espionage saga. All three episodes tap television history as national history that unfolds in the family spaces where the television sets are located.

The Americans is acutely aware of itself as "good TV." The prestigious rubric of "quality television" and the praise of reviewers recognizing it as such enabled the series to take risks with viewer discomfort and be renewed annually despite low ratings. *The Americans* is also acutely aware of television as the material of history and ideology, not just as a chronicle that reflects historical change but also as part of the lived experience of citizenship and nationhood, what it feels like to be, at once, part of a larger history or institution and part of a family. The show's writers and script coordinators often talked about the importance of television in the show's historical timeline. In the writers' room, the elaborate 1980s timeline on the wall always included television schedules from *TV Guide*, so they knew exactly what time *Fantasy Island* came on TV and that it could be a show watched by Paige at 10:45 p.m. (podcast 3.1). While the concern was historical accuracy, *The Americans* constantly used television to illustrate the Americanization of the Jenningses, as Joe Wlodarz (2019) points out: Paige and Henry grow up watching ads for Hershey's kisses and Calvin Klein jeans, in a striking contrast with the scarcities of Elizabeth's and Philip's childhoods in Moscow.

It's crucial that the children are present in all three of the 1983 meta-television episodes. The uniqueness of *The Americans* as a spy series is that as much as it's about marriage, it's also about families and children. Children are intrinsic to Elizabeth's and Philip's mission as part of their cover. They look like they more authentically belong in the suburbs with kids in tow. But kids don't belong in the violent spy genre, so while they complete the picture of the American family in this series, they also reveal the messiness of what the Cold War actually entailed as a clash of ideologies and values. *The Americans* fights its Cold War in the private spaces of bedrooms and family rooms where we think ideology doesn't reside but where in fact children are dazzled by corporate-sponsored magic and chocolate sold as kisses.

The first of the three meta-television episodes, "March 8, 1983," builds up to the TV news coverage of Reagan's speech to the National Association of Evangelicals on that date. Because the speech was pitched to conservative clergy, Reagan was able to call out the Soviet Union in moral and theological terms not usually used in state rhetoric. Famously dubbing the USSR an "evil empire" and the "focus of evil in the modern world," he criticized antinuke liberals for being oblivious to the Cold War's meaning as "the struggle between right and wrong, good and evil." It was widely interpreted as his position against the nuclear freeze being debated in Congress that would have prevented the use of American cruise and Pershing II missiles in Europe.

In the final moments of this episode, which is the third season's finale, portions of his speech play on the television in the Jenningses' bedroom, where Elizabeth mocks the rosy cheeks of Reagan's makeup and says he looks like a clown. Meanwhile, in her own bedroom, Paige huddles on the phone with Pastor Tim, confiding her parents' identity as Russians working for that very same evil empire. Paige's betrayal is especially disconcerting because Reagan's worldview lays out the Cold War in starkly black-and-white terms: you were either on the side of America or on the side of evil. Paige is an evangelical herself, prone to think in these rigid moral terms, but she's also a traumatized teenager who badly needs adult comfort and guidance. How could we *not* be on her side, the side of an American child whose parents are working for the evil empire?

But *The Americans* has positioned its audience to waffle about this either-or politics. We know the Jenningses are on the wrong side of the Cold War. We abhor their brutality. Philip has just murdered Martha's office associate Gene, and he tells Elizabeth in a shaky voice that Gene's living room was full of toys and games like "the stuff Henry plays with," shockingly tying the murder to his fatherhood and to the innocence of children. In turn, Elizabeth's mockery of Reagan's television makeup rings with an adolescent churlishness. But Reagan's reductive Star Wars rhetoric was likewise adolescent, and it dangerously escalated the possibility of a nuclear war. Elizabeth is right to be appalled by it. And we're further nudged onto her side, rather than Paige's, because we don't want the Jenningses' story to come to a cataclysmic end because of a teenager's angst and bad judgment. The momentum of "good TV" is that we get invested in characters we keep rooting for, and in the case of antihero stories like *Breaking Bad* or *The Americans*, the momentum is a thrill ride. The thrill here, though, perilously careens into viewers' feelings about a vulnerable fifteen-year-old whose desperate call to a pastor is both totally understandable and infuriating. Framing her betrayal within the broadcast of Reagan's "Evil Empire" speech, *The Americans* reminds viewers that the moral ground of this series is a minefield, and as the season 3 cliffhanger, it dangles Paige as the collateral damage.

We see this damage in the "David Copperfield" episode that takes place a month later and more than halfway into season 4. It includes Copperfield's preface speech, which unabashedly uses Cold War language to justify the exploitation of a beloved national symbol for commercial television. Copperfield piously explains that this spectacle demonstrates "how precious our liberty is and how easily it can be lost" lest we preserve it by "thinking and speaking and acting as free human beings." His pitch clearly mimics the escalated Cold War rhetoric characterizing the Soviet Union as a looming threat to freedom—indeed, an evil empire. It's the second spiel on freedom that we hear in this episode of *The Americans*. Earlier, an EST instructor harangues his seminar audience—which includes Elizabeth—about how everyone has the opportunity "to live an authentic life" by stepping out of the boxes and traps we create for ourselves. Elizabeth is visibly unnerved by the challenge that she has the freedom to change her life, though her feedback to Philip is that it was a way to sell more seminars.

But the Copperfield stunt seems to reel her in. Watching it on the chunky TV set in the family room, Elizabeth and Philip are as entranced as Henry and Paige, part of a national audience drawn together around a large-scale illusion. *The Americans* episode pushes the theme of illusion by cutting from the Jenningses watching the television special to the Jenningses seven months later, again looking like a happy suburban family. Philip and Elizabeth play hockey with Henry in the driveway while Paige plays miniature golf with Pastor Tim and his wife, pausing at a small cheesy replica of the Statue of Liberty on the green—a clue about the hollowness of grand symbolism and Copperfield's bombast. The hollowness of this entire family picture is revealed when Paige returns and sullenly reports to her parents on what the couple had been doing and talking about. After she had confided to the pastor that her parents are Russian spies, the Jenningses lied to him that their mission was "peace work," so now it's her job to perform as the well-adjusted daughter of human-rights activists and to make reports to her parents on how well that ruse is going. Paige is learning that free choices have consequences. The EST instructor might tell her it's a trap of her own making, but he'd be hard pressed to tell her how to step out of it or how "to live an authentic life" without sending her parents to prison. Along the same lines, Copperfield's jingoism about "thinking and speaking and acting as free human beings" falls flat against Paige's misery. Leveraging a moment of "good TV"—the Statue of Liberty special—against the entrapment of a depressed fifteen-year-old is also achingly good TV.

Before she herself is recruited to the KGB, Paige becomes an unwilling spy for her parents, reporting on her time spent with Pastor Tim.

Personal and national histories are likewise interlocked in *The Americans*' episode structured around the November 1983 television special *The Day After* ("The Day After" 4.9). The made-for-TV movie dramatized a nuclear war between the United States and the Soviet Union by showing its effects on families in the American Midwest. It set a ratings record for viewership and made an impact even at the White House, where the telephone switchboard was overwhelmed with calls. Reagan himself wrote in his diary that he was affected by this film.[2] In *The Americans* episode, its representation begins not with the movie but with its introduction by one of its actors, John Cullum, who advises that parents watch it with their children so it can be discussed responsibly. The content warning acknowledges the jolting effects of *The Day After* in depicting nuclear war through stories of parents and children, uncannily mirroring *The Americans*' depiction

2 In his diary Ronald Reagan (1983) noted after an advanced screening that the film was "very effective & left me very depressed." Also see Deron Overpeck (2012) on the larger cultural reactions to this television event.

of Cold War violence through stories of family melodrama. Family TV with a content warning is, strikingly, a way to describe both shows.

In fact, shots from the two fictional shows are edited together as a way to make this point, showing horrific scenes from *The Day After* and horrified viewers from *The Americans*—the Jennings family, Stan and his son, Young Hee and Don. We see the stunned Russian spectators as well: embassy chief Arkady Zotov; Oleg with his new lover, Tatiana (Vera Cherny); and the Jenningses' KGB colleague William Crandall (Dylan Baker), a fellow illegal. *The Day After* relentlessly spells out one possible outcome of Cold War escalation: all of them—not just the KGB and the FBI but everyone they know and love—annihilated. Once again, Paige is the character who most vividly registers the horror of being in a family where the Cold War is fought at home. Upset by what she's seen, she seeks out Philip, who assures her that he and her mother are working to make sure a nuclear holocaust doesn't happen. But when Paige presses him on it, asking if their work will actually make a difference, he admits he doesn't know. So while the inclusion of *The Day After* dramatizes the stakes of *The Americans*' spy-versus-spy narrative, the conversation between Paige and Philip also blatantly undercuts its protagonists, whose Cold War missions like the exploitation of Martha may have no effect at all.

But that kind of nihilism about meaningful human action is too dark for the essential Americanism of this series, evident in the closure to *The Day After* thread in this episode. Still disturbed by the holocaust portrayed in the TV movie, Oleg tells Tatiana about a hushed-up recent incident when faulty Soviet technology nearly sparked just such a disaster. He's referring to the real-life event of September 26, 1983, when the Soviet early-detection system mistakenly reported incoming American missiles, which would have triggered a nuclear counterattack. But a Soviet air-defense officer, Stanislav Petrov, made the correct guess that given the small number of missiles showing up on the radar, it was probably a Soviet computer malfunction. "Against all his orders and training," says Oleg, the officer made a judgment call and treated it as a false alarm. Telling the story to Tatiana, Oleg muses about what he would have done if he were that officer in charge. Throughout the series, Oleg has been portrayed as exactly such an officer who, we imagine, likewise would have defied orders and made the right call, and in fact Oleg makes excruciating ethical choices in the final season that lead to his American imprisonment.

Petrov was dismissed from the Soviet military on the grounds he'd failed to log in a report, and he lived a life of obscurity, poverty, and mental illness until his story surfaced more than a decade later, years after the Soviet Union had collapsed. He was eventually honored in Western Europe and in the United States, and he was the subject of a Danish documentary, *The Man Who Saved the World* (2014) that included his visit with his movie hero, Kevin Costner. On the day Petrov was honored by the United Nations in New York, the Russians issued a statement that no single person could possibly have made such a serious decision about a nuclear counterattack because other systems and intelligence data would have been checked first. But *The Americans* springs from the same heroic storytelling mode as *The Man Who Saved the World*, despite Philip's admission that the effects of his work may total to nothing at all. By the end of the series, both Philip and Elizabeth make the right call by turning against the KGB, and although their choices don't dramatically change Cold War history, they're what we expect of protagonists in American television.

Cold War Americans

So what's pictured and what's excluded in *The Americans*' TV family and milieu? We don't see any Black families in the Jenningses' neighborhood, but we see young Henry doing imitations of Eddie Murphy from *Saturday Night Live*, and we see police violence against a Black man when Gregory's death is reported on TV while Elizabeth is making dinner. *The Americans*' focus on the white, heterosexual, middle-class family reflects how race played out, generally, on 1980s television, through Black supporting characters whose story lines rarely involved racial issues except for the television trope of "a very special episode" or two, like the Gregory story line of season 1. The series seems to acknowledge that Gregory may have been used that way when Elizabeth herself uses his story to convince Paige that the Soviets are trying to do good in America. She takes Paige to Gregory's neighborhood and tells her that she and Philip had been involved in the civil rights movement when they first came to the United States ("Walter Taffet," 3.7) It's a cringe moment because while Elizabeth's feelings about both racism and Gregory may be sincere, her implication that the KGB's work is entirely humanitarian is disingenuous. In the same episode, a racist South African intelligence officer gets one of the series' worst executions—burned to death with a car tire around him—in a high-profile slapdown of racism, showing where the series stands on this.

But while the scarcity of racial diversity and lack of attention to race on *The Americans* may align with the look of 1980s television, it also aligns, more alarmingly, to the look of contemporary "quality TV," which, with a few notable exceptions, tilts toward white protagonists and scenarios. The Gregory subplot occurs early in the series, and a more serious engagement with race and racism doesn't occur until the South African subplot of season 3. This is also when the series introduces its only recurring Black character, Stan's FBI counterintelligence partner Dennis Aderholt (Brandon J. Dirden). Aderholt shows up in some routine appearances with Gaad, but in his first serious scene with Stan, he's portrayed in a light we don't see afterward, aggressively challenging Stan about his previous assignment undercover in an Arkansas white supremacy group. He asks Stan how he managed to "fool" them, and his tone makes clear that he's deeply suspicious of a white man who's only *pretending* to be a racist. Stan replies that you mimic people and give them what they want to hear—exactly the strategy that allows Philip and Elizabeth to fit in to suburban Virginia ("Open House" 3.3).

Aderholt never gets his own "very special episode" nor a lot of development, though by the end of the series, he's risen through the

Agent Aderholt (Brandon J. Dirden) challenges Stan Beeman about working with white supremacists in an undercover assignment.

ranks and has been promoted to director of counterintelligence, a move that would actually have been unlikely in the FBI of that era. Commenting on how he played the role, Dirden said he often thought of his own father working as a professional in the 1980s and being aware he had to be far more competent than his white colleagues. Dirden also said he researched the culture of the FBI during that time, when it was hit with a number of lawsuits for discrimination (podcast 6.9). The troubled history of integration in federal agencies had gotten national attention with Sam Greenlee's 1969 best-selling novel, *The Spook Who Sat by the Door*, which imagines the first Black CIA officer, who is treated badly and later uses the agency's own tactics against it. The title, which plays on the racial slur that's also a slang word for spy, refers to the cynical business or government practice of hiring just one Black person who's given a desk in a prominent office location for good Affirmative Action optics.

The most skeptical reading of Aderholt is that he's the "spook at the door," prominent in scenes at the FBI but serving mostly as Stan's office buddy. But Aderholt is the one who makes the final breakthrough in the investigation of the Jenningses by convincing the Russian Orthodox priest to give them up in the series finale. Dirden says he played that scene by using Aderholt's faith in America as the way to appeal to the priest's faith in God, convincing him that what's at stake is larger than either of them. "Aderholt has extreme faith in the United States of America. . . . He's totally bought into this idea that everybody can be equal," even though "the American dream has failed people who look like me," Dirden comments (podcast 6.10). The Jenningses themselves are the standard cultural picture of what the American dream looks like, an optics that's wholly an illusion, but Aderholt acquires a wife and baby by season 6 and is actually the only character whose family is intact by the end of the series.

"A couple kids. American dream. You'd never suspect them. She's pretty. He's lucky." That's the description of the Jenningses murmured to Stan and Aderholt by the Soviet illegal William Crandall in his final delirious moments. He's dying of Lassa, a fatal virus that he intended to hand over to the KGB; he injects it into himself when he realizes he's going to be caught by the FBI ("Persona Non Grata" 4.13). It will take Stan years to realize that the pretty wife is Elizabeth, and the lucky guy is his dear friend, Philip, heading the American dream family across the street. William himself is one of the unluckiest characters on the series. His twenty-five years as an illegal and his experience as a chemist have been mostly wasted, and he's deeply disaffected with his mission and with the KGB. He and his KGB partner were supposed to have posed as a suburban couple—like the Jenningses—and become a family, but she left him and went back to the Soviet Union. He regards the Jenningses with envy and bitterness, to the point that they haunt his dying hour, when he mumbles about them to Stan and Aderholt.

But William is a haunting figure too. Marginalized and lonely, William may also represent, in his gruesome death, an issue faced by another marginalized population in the 1980s—AIDS, the social issue of the era that *The Americans* elides.[3] Talking about their careful plotting of the series in relation to historical events, the showrunners said that even though major historical events crossed their timeline, they sometimes did not include them—the shooting down of the Korean airliner in 1983, for instance—because "it's not where the characters went" (podcast 4.1). But the characters did in fact go there—to LGBTQ issues—with the season 2 subplot of Andrew Larrick (Lee Tergesen), a former US Navy SEAL who was being blackmailed because of his homosexuality. Larrick appears in the episodes taking place beginning in March 1982. The new disease named acquired immunodeficiency syndrome had been getting national attention for the previous eight months. The first national CDC (Centers for Disease Control and Prevention) conference on AIDS took place in September 1981, and gay advocacy began soon thereafter; the Gay Men's Health Crisis service was founded in January 1982. AIDS had become a significant enough cultural presence to be represented on television for the first time in 1983 on an episode of *St. Elsewhere* (NBC 1982–88) during its second season. It was also an issue in the real-life story of Jack Barsky, the high-profile Soviet illegal who dropped out of the KGB in 1988 by falsely reporting he had AIDS. He calculated correctly that Soviet fear of HIV/AIDS was so powerful that they wouldn't pursue him. They told his wife in Germany that he was dead (Barsky 2017, 252–53).

The virus story that *The Americans* instead engages is the one about a possible bioweapon, Lassa, which resembles Ebola in its symptoms. Thinking of William's death as an evocation of AIDS may be a poetic reading, but his lonely death hauntingly represents all those who feel marginalized in a culture in which the Jenningses represent the prototype citizens and subjects—a white, middle-class, nuclear family. William talks on his deathbed of feeling isolated and invisible. Philip and Elizabeth, no matter how besieged and even suffering the losses of their children at the end of the series, are easier to picture

3 This interpretation is offered by Pignetti (2019).

as cultural ideals. She's beautiful. He's lucky. In the casting dynamics that still demand a more traditionally attractive wife, they are the television couple most likely to appear on our screens. But as violent KGB agents, they are also a profoundly unlikely TV couple, and placing their espionage stories inside a suburban family remains a unique and considerable achievement of *The Americans*.

Cold War Children

The Americans dismantles the sentimentality of family TV by revealing the ways children are absorbed into adult agendas and ideologies. Though television espionage drama has always been attentive to the anxieties, romances, and "inner feelings" of its spy characters, to use the words of the Russian illegal Andrei Bezrukov (Corera 2020, 310), those dramas had previously excluded the domestic stories of parenting and children. But *The Americans* focuses on spies whose credibility depends on them being part of a family, an ideological touchstone in Reagan's family-values America and an enduring topos mobilized by television's homeliest and home-centered genre, the domestic melodrama.

The story lines about children and parenthood galvanize *The Americans*' harshest critiques of the Jenningses and the KGB illegals program. One of the series' most abhorrent subplots is Philip's exploitation of Kimmy, who's the same age as Paige, offering worrisome scenes of a sleazily disguised Philip flirting with a clueless teenager. Kimmy's father is a CIA operative, and Philip is able to insinuate himself into Kimmy's life and house by playing the hip older counterculture guy intensely interested in a fifteen-year-old's problems. Lonely and flattered by his attention, Kimmy confides in "Jim" far more than Paige can confide in Philip, so the sadness of Kimmy's story reflects the sadness of Philip's dishonesty and failures as a parent. There's also the cringe factor. He carefully avoids sex with Kimmy until the final season, as the previous chapter points out, when Elizabeth manipulates him into it—a moral low point for the Jenningses and a powerful indictment of KGB tactics.

But while Kimmy's story reveals a teenager thoroughly deceived by adult agendas, other teenagers on *The Americans* play far more chilling roles in this series' fearless exposé of children as the heirs of national ideologies. In season 2, adolescent Jared Connors (Owen Campbell) kills his sister and his parents, who are KGB illegals like the Jenningses, posing as a suburban family. Jared murders them in a quarrel because they don't want him involved in the second-generation illegals program for which he'd already been recruited. "What we do, it's for something greater than ourselves," he explains to Elizabeth and Philip about the killings, while he himself is dying of gunshot wounds ("Echo" 2.13). Viewers realize he's mimicking the jargon of his KGB recruiter, with whom he's fallen in love; he murdered his family so he and she could be KGB agents together. Elizabeth uses similarly canned language when she explains herself to Betty, the elderly woman she kills. She's committing the murder "to make the world a better place," she says, certainly a phrase and concept that was a part of everyday life growing up in the postwar Soviet Union. So the puppy love tied up with Jared's ideological fervor lays bare the emotional basis of our ideas and loyalties, how much their intellectual content is shaped by who we love and where we live. The Jenningses are spooked by Jared's ability to murder his own family but far less by his zealotry, given they themselves were teenagers when they joined the KGB. The revelation about Jared isn't enough to stop Elizabeth from guiding her own daughter into the same second-generation illegals program.

The season 5 story of Tuan Eckert (Ivan Mok), a Vietnamese teenager orphaned in the American war there, similarly depicts adolescent espionage ambition gone wrong. Embittered toward Americans, Tuan works for the Vietnamese government on a joint mission with the KGB, and the Jenningses pose as his adoptive parents, the Eckerts, in order to spy on the nearby family of a Soviet defector. As a fictional, Soviet-constructed family, the Eckerts are doppelgangers of the Jenningses themselves, but this time "playing parents to a kid who's so much more like them" than their own children, as the showrunners remarked (podcast 5.2). Trying to help with the assignment, Tuan coaches the defector's teenage son in an ill-advised fake suicide attempt that's nearly fatal ("The World Council of Churches" 5.12). Again, while truly shaken by Tuan's bad judgment and the narrowly averted tragedy, Elizabeth continues to encourage Paige on the same radicalized path.

This is the radical path of *The Americans* itself in staking out the family as the scene of the ideological recruitment of children. The exploitation of *The Americans*' teenagers resonates with the moral repugnance of child abuse, and the series' bluntest criticism of the Jenningses in fact hones in on the indecency of what they're doing to Paige by implicating her in their politics and spy work. Early in the fifth season, Philip and Elizabeth literally stumble upon the depths of Paige's trauma when they find her curled up asleep in her bedroom closet, apparently the only place where she can feel safe ("Pests" 5.2).

Later that season, a far more direct condemnation emerges through the words of Pastor Tim. Paige has stealthily photographed pages from the pastor's journal, which her parents develop in a

The story of Vietnamese teenager Tuan Eckert (Ivan Mok) illustrates *The Americans*' radical use of children in espionage narratives.

makeshift darkroom set up in their basement. Close-ups of the pages reveal descriptions of their bad parenting in stark terms: "Are they monsters? I don't know. But what they did to their daughter, I'd have to call monstrous. I've seen sexual abuse, I've seen affairs. But nothing I've seen compares to what [Paige] has been through. . . . She doesn't even know how much she's suffering" ("Darkroom" 5.10). Are they monsters? We see Elizabeth, Philip, and Paige reading the pages, stricken, in the ghastly red glow of the darkroom safelight that washes the entire basement scene in horror-film hues, a scathing judgment on Philip and Elizabeth's absorption of Paige into their dark world.

The recruitment of Paige, Tuan, and Jared into the illegals program is described by Claudia in socialist terms repellent to most Americans. "Paige is your daughter, but she's not just yours," Claudia tells their parents earlier in the series. "She belongs to the cause and to the world. We all do. You haven't forgotten that, have you?" ("Echo" 2.13). Her remark is geared to outrage our traditional ideas about children belonging to families. But *The Americans* slyly complicates this reaction by showing Paige's recruitment into the far less threatening and in fact family-friendly worlds of evangelical religion and Christian left-wing activism. Paige is recruited into Pastor Tim's church by another teenager, Kelli (Lizzy DeClement), who spots Paige as a vulnerable target and pretends to understand her completely ("The Walk In" 2.3). Later, Kelli leads Paige to a church that persuades her to donate all her allowance money to its missions. Paige secretly meets up with Kelli and the church group in the same episode in which Elizabeth and Philip discuss whether or not one of their contacts is "recruitable" ("A Little Night Music" 2.4).

The story of Paige's enlistment into evangelical Christianity happens at the same time the Jenningses are dealing with Jared and then learning the terrible truth that he was the one who murdered his family because of his commitment to the illegals program. By the end of that season, Paige is committed, too, having gone to an antinuke demonstration where Pastor Tim was arrested for civil disobedience. "This moved me," she explains to her parents, because it made her realize that Christianity is about self-sacrifice for "the greater good." The title of this episode is "Echo" (2.13), the name of a computer system that can test stealth missile designs, but it also describes how Paige sounds a lot like Jared, who similarly exclaimed about working for "something greater than ourselves." Even more alarmingly, Jared's words mimic those of Elizabeth who, not yet knowing Jared was their killer, told him that his parents were admirable because "they believed in something greater than themselves." Claudia's rebuke about children belonging to "the cause" appears in this episode too. The altruistic appeal grows more and more hollow as it resounds across generations and ideologies.

The Americans doesn't equate evangelical Christianity and the KGB illegals program, nor Paige's secrets and lies with those of Jared or the Jenningses. Philip's stern lecture to her—"Lying will not be tolerated"—is outrageous because of the massively larger scope of Philip's own lies and deceptions. But *The Americans* makes a point about teenagers being recruitable in their loneliness and in their yearning to belong, to matter, and to become emotionally drawn into a cause: "It moved me," Paige says.

Elizabeth venting about Paige's religious conversion—"This is what happens! They get them while they're children!" ("A Little Night Music" 2.4)—is especially ironic because the series keeps reminding us of the parallels with Elizabeth's recruitment as a young girl in Moscow, naive and hopeful. She was only a little older than Paige when she was raped by her KGB trainer, a red flag, so to speak, about how young people devoted to a cause can be mistreated by the authorities they trust. There's no hint of abuse by the pastor or any adults in the church, though Pastor Tim is a smug, vaguely unlikable character who comes perilously close to being killed off. As they did with Martha, the writers play a mean game of chicken in taunting viewers about the appeal and likelihood of this happening. Ironically, Pastor Tim is vindicated in the end when, unlike Russian Orthodox Father Andrei, he doesn't cave to the FBI's questions about the Jenningses. Yet the bottom line is that Pastor Tim stands for something ostensibly admirable—a pastor guiding children and young people to social-justice work—and the fact that this becomes creepy speaks to *The Americans'* deep suspicions about susceptibility to ideology.

Showrunners Weisberg and Fields found it "very upsetting" that a number of fans wanted Paige to die, too, perceiving her, like Pastor Tim, as an irritating threat to the Jenningses (Wittmer 2018). But a kill-Paige campaign isn't surprising given the unsentimental portrayal of children in *The Americans*. At the start of season 2, Paige walks into her parents' bedroom without knocking and finds them in fellatio—a savvy metaphor for the kids in this series stumbling into adult scenarios but startling because television dramas rarely depict parents' sex lives in relationship to their children ("Comrades" 2.1). *The Americans* unflinchingly situates children in dangerous proximity to adult activities steeped in deception and violence, including grimy histories of lovers, honey-trap marks, and a parallel marriage with another wife. In a similarly unsettling incident in season 6, Philip harshly proves to Paige that she's grown overconfident in her martial-arts skills, putting her into a series of humiliating chokeholds that brutally literalize tough love ("The Great Patriotic War" 6.5). No matter how empowered Paige may feel about being in the illegals program, the slapdown coldly demonstrates how little power she actually wields in the dangerous world she's entered. There's no happy ending for any of the Cold War children on *The Americans*, including Philip's Russian son, Mischa (Alex Ozerov), whose plan to meet his father in the United States is foiled by the KGB. Philip's other son, Henry, will clearly be damaged by his parents' abandonment no matter how lovingly Stan takes him on as a surrogate son.

These disturbing stories about children and parent-child relationships enact *The Americans'* skepticism about "family TV" by representing the complications of parenthood, the inner lives of children, and the infusion of ideologies into everyday family life. Perhaps the final irony in conveying an espionage story through stories of parents and children is that Stan Beeman nails the Jenningses not through his FBI investigations but through sweetly oblivious Henry, who casually shares the observation that his parents are always coming and going in the middle of the night. It's the piece of information that makes Stan suddenly see what he'd refused to see for six years and now learns through a high-school boy. But the final thrust against a sentimental view of children comes toward the end of the series finale, when Elizabeth, asleep on the plane to Moscow, dreams that she's in bed with her lover Gregory, having a postcoital cigarette. When he points to her belly and obvious pregnancy, she says, "I never wanted children anyway," and then her eyes drift to a portrait of Paige and Henry near the bed. The kids have been there all along, brought up as Americans.

Little wonder, then, that Paige is aghast, at the end of the series, to be told by her parents that they've been discovered by the FBI and have to go "home." "To Russia?" Paige cries. And given the importance of children in this series—as victims, perpetrators, innocent witnesses, and most of all as passionately loved family members—their concluding stories carry all the emotional weight of the series finale. The knockout punches of *The Americans* are the losses of the Jenningses' children. In a devastating scene, they phone Henry at boarding school from a public telephone to hear his voice and tell him they love him one last time before they abandon him. But at least they've made the hard choice to do this; far worse is that Paige gives them no choice at all in her decision to split from her parents and remain in the United States.

The scene depicting Paige's decision is crafted around the suspense of the previous moments on the train to Canada when the border policeman studied the couple's fake passports and compared them to artist sketches of the FBI fugitives. It's a bittersweet reminder of Stan staring at similar sketches and not seeing what's in front of him. In the relief of having Philip and Elizabeth pass the scrutiny, viewers may not realize there are no shots of the border police doing the same with Paige. The train pulls out of the station, and the camera reveals Elizabeth and then Philip, in the next car, stunned to see Paige standing on the platform. Standing perfectly still and watching her parents transported out of her life, she moves across the viewer's screen as the train passes her by. It's perfect metaphor of the Jenningses' powerlessness: the train's relentless movement into a future without their children and the large window like a movie screen picturing what they'd feared most. Philip walks to the next car to share his grief with Elizabeth, but they can only sit with their sorrow in silence, shaking, not touching, willing their faces to control their tears. Reviewers and the actors themselves commented that, more than imprisonment or execution, the loss of their children is a fitting punishment for the atrocities Elizabeth and Philip have committed throughout the series. But Paige and Henry are the "real" Americans of the series' title. They're simply staying home.

The Jenningses are the real thing, *The Americans* suggests in its finale, because their bonding is no longer espionage and shared missions but parenthood, marriage, and home—the traditional themes of domestic melodrama. The episode's last scene offers a rhapsodized version of all three. Following their anguished loss of Paige and their long journey back to the USSR, Elizabeth and Philip stand on an overlook far above the snow and glittering lights of Moscow, talking about their children and what life may have been like had they not been "Americans" for the past decades. They wonder if they could have been workers who met on a bus—a fantasy that they may have been fated for each other even if the KGB hadn't assigned them together. Moscow itself is likewise romanticized from this height and distance, a contrast to the gritty close-ups of everyday life there that we'd seen in previous episodes—the bare shelves in the supermarket where Martha had been looking for food, the policing of food supply chains by a dejected Oleg. When Philip admits that this homecoming "feels strange," Elizabeth replies in Russian, "We'll get used to it."

No longer Americans, Mikhail and Nadezhda look over the lights of Moscow, which now is home.

The return to home is a central trope in melodrama's prioritizing of private space and private life. It's a sharp contrast to Elizabeth's and Philip's stories as Soviet citizens, doing public service by setting up an ersatz "home" in the American suburbs. But *The Americans* had always undermined this premise by centralizing the emotional dynamics of home life as the real thing and the real topic of this series. In an earlier scene in the finale, we see the Jenningses' house transformed into a crime scene, their belongings carried out in boxes by Stan's FBI colleagues. But that doesn't matter. "Home" has moved to where the Jenningses are now, "where the heart is," as the proverb goes, where they return as Nadezhda and Mikhail.

Earlier, the series finale had movingly used two 1980s rock songs in montages to portray the losses of home, family, and bromance. Over shots of the departing Jennings, the diminished Stan, and the imprisoned Oleg, we hear Dire Straits' "Brothers in Arms," a plaintive ballad about the loneliness of soldiers returning after war, isolated from their comrades but also from the people at home. The song's last lines surprisingly reveal that the "brothers in arms" include the enemy they were fighting: "We're fools to make war / On our brothers in arms," a wholly fitting coda to this Cold War story of Americans versus "Americans." The following song, U2's "With or without You," plays during the border scenes; we hear the agonized chorus, "I can't live, I can't live," as we watch Elizabeth and Philip on the train seeing Paige vanish from their lives.

Tellingly, *The Americans*' final musical piece, played during their journey back to the USSR in the last scene, departs from this playlist, which had woven the series into 1980s Cold War history. We instead hear classical Russian music, Tchaikovsky's op. 6, no. 6, which removes Philip and Elizabeth from that history altogether and folds them into the more emotional history of Russia as home. The music plays through the final shot of the couple in silhouette above Moscow's sparkling lights, filling the air, in Jonathan Goldberg's terms, with melodrama's dissolution of boundaries and rigid identities.

Viewers know, as the Jenningses cannot imagine at this moment, that the Soviet Union will dissipate in a few years, the borders will open, the Iron Curtain will fall, and their violent efforts to take down the United States will have sunken into a larger secret history. Will they be able to see their children again? Or will Paige have been swept up by FBI counterintelligence like the real-life illegals Jack Barsky and Andrei Bezrukov? In Moscow, will Mikhail run across Martha in a park with her adopted child? The pleasure of imagining these fictional futures suggests how much we as viewers want to linger in the world of *The Americans* where history and fiction intermingle in seductive and compelling ways.

WORKS CITED

Alston, Joshua. 2016. "*The Americans* Music Supervisor on Building Tension with Music from the Cold War '80s." AV Club. March 15, 2016. tv.avclub.com/the-americans-music-supervisor-on-building-tension-wit-1798245204.

Amami, Gazelle. 2016. "*The Americans*' Alison Wright on the Tragedy of Playing Martha." Vulture. March 15, 2016. www.vulture.com/2016/03/martha-the-americans-alison-wright.html.

Andrew, Christopher, and Vasili Mitrokhin. 1999. *The Sword and the Shield: The Mitrokhin Archive and the Secret History of the KGB*. New York: Basic Books.

Armstrong, Olivia. 2015. "The Grey Area: Exploring Sex and Marriage in 'The Americans.'" Decider. January 26, 2015. decider.com/2015/01/26/the-americans-fx-marriage/.

Barsky, Jack. 2017. *Deep Undercover: My Secret Life & Tangled Allegiances as a KGB Spy in America*. Carol Stream, IL: Tyndale Momentum.

Bastién, Angelica Jade. 2018. "The Blistering Vulnerability of *The Americans* Finale's Garage Scene." Vulture. May 31, 2018. www.vulture.com/2018/05/the-americans-finale-parking-garage-scene.html.

Borenstein, Eliot. 2016. "Perestroika Blues." Public Books. June 2, 2016. www.publicbooks.org/author/eliot-borenstein/.

Brooks, Peter. 1976. *The Melodramatic Imagination: Balzac, Henry James, Melodrama and the Mode of Excess*. New Haven, CT: Yale University Press.

Collins, Laura. 2014. "The Spy Who Loved Me." *New Yorker*, August 18, 2014. www.newyorker.com/magazine/2014/08/25/the-spy-who-loved-me-2.

Corera, Gordon. 2020. *Russians among Us: Sleeper Cells, Ghost Stories, and the Hunt for Putin's Spies*. New York: William Morrow.

DeAngelis, Michael. 2014. "Introduction." In *Reading the Bromance: Homosocial Relations in Film and Television*, edited by Michael DeAngelis, 1–26. Detroit: Wayne State University Press.

Egner, Jeremy. 2018. "Margo Martindale on 'The Americans' and Life as an 'Esteemed Character Actress.'" *New York Times*, May 23, 2018.

Friedlander, Whitney. 2018. "'The Americans' Bosses on Pivotal Series Finale Scene as Exploration of 'Six Seasons' Worth of a Real Relationship." *Variety*, May 30, 2018. variety.com/2018/tv/features/the-americans-series-finale-interview-spoilers-1202824832/.

Gessen, Masha. 2018. "Translating 'The Americans,' and Seeing a Mirror of My Own American Experience." *New Yorker*, June 1, 2018. www.newyorker.com/news/our-columnists/translating-the-americans-and-seeing-a-mirror-of-my-own-american-experience.

Gledhill, Christine. 2018. "Prologue: The Reach of Melodrama." In *Melodrama Unbound: Across History, Media, and National Cultures*, edited by Christine Gledhill and Linda Williams, ix–xxv. New York: Columbia University Press.

Goldberg, Jonathan. 2016. *Melodrama: An Aesthetics of Impossibility*. Durham, NC: Duke University Press.

Goldstein, Jessica M. 2016. "Alison Wright on Martha Hanson's Fate." *Esquire*, May 5, 2016. www.esquire.com/entertainment/tv/q-and-a/a44588/alison-wright-the-americans-interview/.

Greenlee, Stan. 1969. *The Spook Who Sat by the Door*. London: Allison & Busby.

Hagelin, Sarah, and Gillian Silverman. 2022. *The New Female Antiheroes: The Disruptive Women of Twenty-First Century US Television*. Chicago: University of Chicago Press.

Hale, Mike. 2016. "'The Americans,' Season 4, Episode 6: Can Anyone Be Trusted?" *New York Times*, April 20, 2016.

Halperin, Shirley. 2018. "'The Americans' Music Supervisors Pick Their 10 Favorite Song Cues." *Variety*, March 20, 2018. variety.com/2018/music/news/the-americans-music-supervision-songs-1202730700/.

Haskell, Molly. 1999. "The Woman's Film." In *Feminist Film Theory: A Reader*, edited by Sue Thornham, 20–30. New York: New York University Press.

Heller, Karen. 2017. "Martha Is Back on 'The Americans,' and Alison Wright Has Finally Arrived." *Washington Post*, May 3, 2017. www.washingtonpost.com/lifestyle/style/martha-is-back-on-the-americans-and-alison-wright-has-finally-arrived/2017/05/02/22b625c8-2ec7-11e7-9dec-764dc781686f_story.html.

Hibberd, James. 2016. "The Americans Showrunners Explain that Shocking Death." *Entertainment Weekly*, April 6, 2016. ew.com/article/2016/04/06/americans-nina-dead/.

Holson, Laura M. 2013. "The Dark Stuff Distilled." *New York Times*, March 29, 2013.

Jenkins, Tricia. 2009. "The Suburban Spy and the Rise of the New Right: Negotiating Gender Politics in *Scarecrow and Mrs. King*." *Journal of Popular Film & Television* 36 (4): 200–7.

Karlyn, Kathleen. 1995. "Comedy, Melodrama, and Gender: Theorizing the Genres of Laughter." In *Classical Hollywood Comedies*, edited by Kristine Brunovska Karnick and Henry Jenkins, 39–59. New York: Routledge.

Keller, Joel. 2016. "How 'The Americans' Keeps the Jennings Family Real." Fast Company. March 16, 2016. www.fastcompany.com/3057874/how-the-americans-keeps-the-jennings-family-real.

Kreindler, Sarv. 2013. "Cold War Cinematography: Concealing and Revealing on FX's Spy Drama 'The Americans.'" Creative Planet Network. February 6, 2013. Accessed May 23, 2019 (no longer available).

Levine, Elana. 2018. "Melodrama and Soap Opera." *Feminist Media Histories* 4 (2): 117–22.

Liviu-Marius, Bejenaru, 2013. "România Anilor '80 în Optica Lectorilor Americani de la Universitatea 'Alexandru Ioan Cuza' din Iaşi." *Revista de Istorie a Moldovei* 4 (96): 65–82.

Lynch, Jason. 2018. "FX Considered Making The Americans a Broader Show. Instead, It Became a Better One." *AdWeek*, February 28, 2018. www.adweek.com/tv-video/fx-considered-making-the-americans-a-broader-show-instead-it-became-a-better-one/.

Lyons, Margaret. 2013. "TV's Saddest Character: Martha on The Americans." Vulture. May 1, 2013. www.vulture.com/2013/05/the-americans-martha-saddest-character.html.

McGreal, Chris. 2010. "FBI Breaks up Alleged Russian Spy Ring in Deep Cover." *Guardian*, June 28, 2010. www.theguardian.com/world/2010/jun/29/fbi-breaks-up-alleged-russian-spy-ring-deep-cover.

Mizejewski, Linda. 1987. "The Erotic Stripped Bare." *Harper's Magazine*, March 1987, 57–62.

Modleski, Tania. 2010. "Clint Eastwood and Male Weepies." *American Literary History* 22 (1): 136–58.

Muñoz-González, Esther. 2018. "The Americans: Domesticity and Regendering of Classical Spy Narratives." *Brno Studies in English* 44 (1): 119–36.

Nussbaum, Emily. 2015. "'The Americans' Is Too Bleak and That's Why It's Great." *New Yorker*, March 18, 2015. www.newyorker.com/culture/culture-desk/the-americans-is-too-bleak-and-thats-why-its-great.

O'Falt, Chris. 2017. "'The Americans' Turns Brooklyn into an 80s World of D.C. Espionage." IndieWire. May 25, 2017. www.indiewire.com/2017/05/americans-fx-cinematography-brooklyn-locations-period-1201832171/.

Overpeck, Deron. 2012. "'Remember! It's Only a Movie!' Expectations and Receptions of *The Day After* (1983)." *Historical Journal of Film, Radio & Television* 32 (2): 267–92.

Pignetti, Daisy. 2019. "'This Must Be the Place I Waited Years to Leave': From Propaganda to Perestroika." Paper presented at the 2019 annual conference of the Society for Cinema and Media Studies, March 2019, Seattle.

Poniewozik, James. 2015. "Review: *The Americans* Puts Mother (and Father) Russia to the Test." *Time*, January 28, 2015. time.com/3683989/the-americans-review-season-3/.

Prudom, Laura. 2013. "'The Americans' Premiere: Keri Russell and Matthew Rhys Talk Sex, Spy Games, and America Vs. Russia." Huffpost. January 1, 2013. www.huffpost.com/entry/the-americans-premiere-keri-russell-matthew-rhys_n_2584664.

Reagan, Ronald. 1983. "White House Diaries." Ronald Reagan Presidential Library. October 10, 1983. www.reaganfoundation.org/ronald-reagan/white-house-diaries/diary-entry-10101983/.

Rice, Andrew. 2017. "The Russians Are Coming! How *The Americans* Became the Most Relevant Drama on TV." *New York Magazine*, March 3, 2017. nymag.com/tags/the-russians-are-coming/.

Robinson, Joanna. 2017a. "*The Americans* Star Explains Tonight's Shocking Cameo." *Vanity Fair*, March 22, 2017. www.vanityfair.com/hollywood/2017/03/the-americans-martha-alive-cameo-season-5-episode-3-the-midges-alison-wright-interview.

——. 2017b. "*Feud* and *The Americans* Star Alison Wright on the 'Punch in the Gut Scene' She Filmed on Election Eve." *Vanity Fair*, March 27, 2017.

www.vanityfair.com/hollywood/2017/03/feud-recap-season-1-episode-4-more-or-less-alison-wright-pauline-interview.

Rosenberg, Alyssa. 2013. "'The Americans' Open Thread: In the Air Tonight." ThinkProgress. January 31, 2013. archive.thinkprogress.org/the-americans-open-thread-in-the-air-tonight-90be99d0f25/.

Rothman, Joshua. 2016. "The Cruel Irony of 'The Americans,'" *New Yorker*, March 16, 2016. www.newyorker.com/culture/culture-desk/the-cruel-irony-of-the-americans.

Rowles, Dustin. 2016. "The Martha Death Watch on 'The Americans' Is the Most Frustrating, Rewarding Storyline on TV." Uproxx. April 28, 2016. uproxx.com/tv/americans-martha/.

Sandberg, Bryn. 2015a. "'The Americans' Star Keri Russell on Season 3: Is It Sexist to Not Recruit Paige?" *Hollywood Reporter*, January 12, 2015. www.hollywoodreporter.com/live-feed/keri-russell-americans-season-3-767924.

———. 2015b. "'The Americans' Star on Lack of Awards: We Haven't Been Sleeping with the Right People." *Hollywood Reporter*, February 18, 2015. https://www.hollywoodreporter.com/tv/tv-news/americans-matthew-rhys-spoilers-awards-774652/.

Saraiya, Sonia. 2015. "The Best TV Show You're Not Watching." Salon. April 22, 2015. www.salon.com/2015/04/22/the_best_tv_show_youre_not_watching_the_americans_will_never_be_must_see_tv_no_matter_how_hard_it_tries/.

Scott, Simon. 2017. "We Are All Martha: Alison Wright on How Her 'Americans' Character Became a Hit." NPR. March 25, 2017. www.kunc.org/2017-03-25/we-are-all-martha-alison-wright-on-how-her-americans-character-became-a-hit.

Shane, Scott, and Charlie Savage. 2010. "In Ordinary Lives, U.S. Sees Work of Russian Agents." *New York Times*, June 28.

Sklar, Robert, and Tania Modleski. 2005. "'Million Dollar Baby': A Split Decision." *Cineaste* 30 (3): 6–11.

State Journal Register. 2013. "FX's The Americans: Spy Thriller or Family Drama?" January 23, 2013. www.sj-r.com/article/20130129/NEWS/301299962?template=ampart.

Tasker, Yvonne. 2002. *Spectacular Bodies: Gender, Genre, and the Action Cinema*. London: Routledge.

Varadi, Anna. 2019. "'Tainted Love,' the Walkman, and Cold-Blooded Murder: The 1980s and FX's *The Americans*." Paper presented at the 2019 annual conference of the Society for Cinema and Media Studies, March 2019, Seattle.

Walker, Shaun. 2016. "The Day We Discovered Our Parents Were Russian Spies." *Guardian*, May 7, 2016. https://www.theguardian.com/world/2016/may/07/discovered-our-parents-were-russian-spies-tim-alex-foley.

White, Rosie. 2007. *Violent Femmes: Women as Spies in Popular Culture*. London: Routledge.

Williams, Linda. 2001. *Playing the Race Card: Melodramas of Black and White from Uncle Tom to O. J. Simpson*. Princeton, NJ: Princeton University Press.

Wittmer, Carrie. 2018. "'The Americans' Creators Share Their Feelings on Ending the Show after 6 Seasons and Reveal the Character Fans Wanted Them to Kill." Business Insider. March 30, 2018. www.businessinsider.com/the-americans-on-fx-creators-discuss-their-feelings-ending-the-show-2018-3.

Wlodarz, Joseph. 2019. "Americanization and Ambient Critique: Television in *The Americans*." Paper presented at the 2019 annual conference of the Society for Cinema and Media Studies, March 2019, Seattle.

Zuckerman, Esther. 2014a. "'The Americans' Wig of the Week: Philip's Clark Disguise." *Atlantic*, March 20, 2014. www.theatlantic.com/culture/archive/2014/03/americans-wig-week-philips-clark-disguise/359375/.

——. 2014b. "'The Americans' Wig of the Week: Finale Edition." *Atlantic*, May 22, 2014. www.theatlantic.com/culture/archive/2014/05/the-americans-wig-of-the-week-finale-edition/371419/.

——. 2014c. "Margo Martindale on 'The Americans' and Making You Read Her Mind." *Atlantic*, May 21, 2014. www.theatlantic.com/culture/archive/2014/05/margo-martindale/371326/.

INDEX

Printed in the USA
CPSIA information can be obtained
at www.ICGtesting.com
LVHW011915040624
782270LV00004B/451

9 780814 347430